A PARALYZING
REDEMPTION

A PARALYZING REDEMPTION

ONE MAN'S JOURNEY FROM BASKETBALL STARDOM TO COMPLETE PARALYSIS AND THE LONG ROAD BACK TO WALKING

Brian Ziegler

CROSSLINK
PUBLISHING

A Paralyzing Redemption: One man's journey from basketball stardom to complete paralysis and the long road back to walking

CrossLink Publishing
www.crosslinkpublishing.com

ISBN 978-1-63357-088-7

Library of Congress Control Number: 2016953707

Contents

Chapter One

SCHOOL DAYZ!

I believe every human being has a life-defining moment; a moment so forceful, so dramatic, and so important it changes one's entire existence forever. I had my experience on May 27, 2000. My old way of living had come to an end, and it was the start of a life I never thought possible, a life I never thought I would want. This is a story about second chances, a story about God's mercy, and a story about Jesus Christ hearing the prayers of a desperate young man and changing his life forever.

I grew up in a small town about 45 miles south of Cleveland, Ohio. Canal Fulton was the kind of town where everybody knew each other, a town where people actually cared about one another. For a young ornery punk kid, it was both a blessing and a curse. No matter what stupid thing I did, my parents would always find out. My mom used to tell me she had spies strategically located around the town, so she always knew what I was doing. I thought she made it up, but looking back she may have hired a few ninjas to keep an eye on my friends and me.

I was blessed to have an amazing family that loved and cared for me. People would sometimes affectionately joke that my parents reminded them of "the perfect duo." My mother Vicky was my biggest supporter. As far back as I can remember she was always there for her kids; she never missed a ball game, she took care of us when we were sick, and dragged our lazy selves to church on Sunday mornings when all we wanted to do was go back to sleep. My father Bill was the kind of dad every little kid dreamed of. He was a hardworking graphics supervisor who spent his free time teaching me how to fish and coaching my little league teams. I also had an older brother David and a little sister named Kristen.

Christmas season was always a special time at the Ziegler house.

As far back as I can remember, I was always playing sports. I lived and died for them. I learned at an early age that winning wasn't everything—it was the only thing. I hated to lose at anything and "I thought" losing was for those weak kids who weren't as good as I was. Sports always came easy to me. I would spend hours with my friends playing basketball at the park or football at the local fire station.

I talk to some people who hated their childhoods. They couldn't wait until they graduated so they could leave their old lives behind in search of a new and more exciting one. Not me! Not me, I loved growing up, especially my high school years. I loved all sports. I developed a deep passion for basketball in the ninth grade. As a freshman I made the varsity team and was seeing limited action in "garbage duty." One week during practice, a high school alumnus came and practiced with our team. This man was fast and quick with the basketball. Somehow I ended up guarding him and tried my best not to get embarrassed. I was determined to "check" him no matter what. He was not going to make me look like a small, weak, scrawny little freshman. I remember seeing the ball bounce up and down in his right hand; if I could time it right I could steal the ball on his crossover. He bounced once, then twice, now a third time; I knew the next dribble would be a switch to his left hand. I stuck my hand out and tipped the ball away from him. He got the ball back and set up the offence again. This time he looked angry. *No way is this little punk going to take the ball again.* He drove right at me and I stole the ball a second time. I couldn't believe it, was this really happening? My coach was ecstatic. He stopped the entire practice and singled me out. He told me I had earned more playing time. In fact, I was going to start the next game.

So here I was, a freshman about to start at guard in a game with a gang of big strong men two to three years older than me. I was completely freaked out. Now, at the time my brother was the star player on our team. He was big and tough and could score a lot of points. The day of the game he found me in the hall and told me not to make any plans for that night because I was going out with him after the game. That sounded really strange to me because my brother had never asked me to go anywhere with him before. He told me he had a date that night after the game. I thought to myself, *Big deal, what does that have to do with me?* The next thing he told me was the start of my infatuation with "high school living" (and probably the reason so many girls hate my guts to this day). My big bro proceeded to drop another bombshell on me: this girl he was taking out had a friend, and like it or not I was going with him. Of course I liked it; I mean the girl was blonde, popular, and a senior—I was loving life! As the hours ticked closer to game time, I don't know what I was more nervous for: the game or the hot date I had afterwards.

Finally 7:30 came and it was game time. I ran out onto the court completely panicked but ready to play. The announcer called my name, "And now starting at guard, freshman # 23, Brian Ziegler!" I was so excited the adrenaline flowing throw my body was ridiculous. I played the game of my life. I was making three pointers, playing defense, and diving for loose balls. The fourth quarter was about to end and we were all tied up: someone needed to make a play for us to pull out the game. I wish I could have told you it was me that made the game winning shot, but "come on, I was just a freshman." It was my brother who won the game for us. He got the ball on the block and muscled his way to the hoop for the game-winning basket. When the game was over, I finished with fifteen points and seven steals, not bad for my first varsity game. Oh, yea, I also had my first real date with that senior hottie—that didn't go as well, but again "come on, I was just a freshman."

The next morning I woke up and looked at the newspaper. The title of our basketball article read: "Brothers Dominate Northwest Win." I was so proud. I couldn't believe my name made the newspaper and my name was right next to my brother's. Looking back, this is probably the point in my life where I began to love myself more than other people. This became a habit for me. Every Saturday morning after our games I would wake up early and run upstairs to see what was written about me in the paper. I wanted to see how many points I scored. I wanted to see what my scoring average was. I wanted to see if any other freshman were getting the opportunity to play on the varsity team. All I cared about was my stats, how I was doing. Funny thing was the only stat I should have been concerned with was my team's wins and losses. But that wasn't important to me. Wins and losses weren't high on my priority list. They weren't going to get my name in the paper. They weren't going to get me popularity and they sure as heck weren't going to get me any more dates with good-looking senior girls. So I began a love affair—a love affair with myself!

League Championship Game – Northwest vs. Canton South

Going strong to the hoop – Northwest vs. Louisville

I continued to live this way for the next three years of my life. Each year my basketball skills got better and better while my people skills got poorer and poorer. On the outside I was "living out my dream." I had everything I ever wanted—friends, recognition, popularity, and girls. But no matter how much success I gained, there always felt like something was missing, like my life was only half complete. I didn't know it at the time but God was starting to work in my life, prepping me for a major life change.

My favorite thing to do on the basketball court – shoot.

At the end of my senior year I had to make a decision on where I was going to go to college. I had a list of about ten to fifteen colleges to choose from. During the year I took multiple visits to different campuses looking to find the college that best fit my skills and lifestyle. I learned a valuable lesson back then: colleges don't care how good of a basketball player you are. If you don't produce in the classroom, you won't get into their university. I was so busy enjoying my high school years that I didn't have time or want to be bothered with schoolwork. I did just enough in the classroom to stay eligible for the season. I also became familiar with something called the NCAA Clearinghouse. In order for me to play basketball at a Division 1 university, I needed to achieve a 2.0 grade point average and get at least an 18 on the ACT. Well, I got the 2.0 but I could not hit the requirement for the ACT. I took it twice and got a 17 both times.

Senior night at Northwest High School with my two biggest fans –
Mom and Dad

So this left me with only three options for the following year. I could go to a prep school, which was basically just going to a fifth year of high school. The problem with this option was there were no prep schools in the state of Ohio. I could sit out a year and then play the following season. This was not an option for me—the thought of not playing basketball for an entire year made me physically ill. My last option was to attend a junior college for two years and then transfer to another university upon completion. I chose the third option; Edison State Community College in Piqua, Ohio, was where I would be spending the next two years of my life.

Chapter Two

MY FIRST APARTMENT

One of the coolest perks of attending Edison State was that I got my own apartment. The school did not have any dorms, so if you lived away from home you needed to secure your own place to live. My parents went down to Piqua a couple months prior and found an apartment close to school for me to live. My excitement was uncontainable. I was eighteen years old with my own apartment living 3 ½ hours from home—life was good, or so I thought. I remember the first night at my new residence. My mother and father had just helped me unpack my things and were getting ready to go back home. I sat at the side of my bed weeping. I missed my house, my friends, and especially my girlfriend who I left back in Canal Fulton. I did not think I could do this. I remember thinking, *Screw this, I'm going back home!* I will never forget what my mom said to me next: Looking straight into my eyes "I know you are scared; your brother had the same look in his eyes when he went away to school. You can do this, Brian." That was all the reassurance I needed; that one little statement convinced me to give this new life a try.

Living on your own at eighteen years old is a big change. I had to learn to cook for myself, clean, and do my own laundry. Since I was a basketball player, they paired us each with a roommate to help offset cost. I had an awesome roommate named Jamie. He was a 6' 6" massively athletic power forward from a small town in Central Ohio. I did not think it was possible for a human being to jump as high as he could. Jamie and I became extremely close real fast. I couldn't have asked for a better roommate. He taught me many things and I am pretty sure without his guidance I would have died of starvation.

There were two other basketball players who lived in the same apartment complex as Jamie and I. They both grew up a good distance away from Edison and had girlfriends back home. Jamie and I spent many nights over at their apartment relaxing after practice. Now, I was not a big drinker in high school but I did have an occasional drink (or two or three). Both of my new friends were only eighteen and nineteen years old but they had IDs that said otherwise. So the four of us started to drink alcohol on a fairly regular basis. At first it was just a few beers, but soon we were drinking massive amounts of beer and liquor. Before I knew it, I was spending most of the money my parents sent me on alcohol and fast food (beer liquor, and fast food.)

Looking back on my first year of college, I have no idea how we survived. We would be up all night drinking then wake up for 6:00 AM workouts, go to class all day, and then have either practice or a game in the evening. We did this every night of the week. We did not think twice about drinking a six-pack and hopping in the car drunk and going to the next party. We had no one to report to and no one to supervise us (besides our coaches.) We were accountable to no one. This was an immense turning point in my life: I became submerged into this lifestyle and there seemed to be no way out.

After my first year of college I came home for the summer and my life returned to some sort of familiarity. I was back in the house with my parents, spending time with my friends, and strengthening my strained relationship with my girlfriend. I was playing basketball all the time. Mom was spoiling me with her amazing cooking and even doing my laundry for me. Everything was good, and life seemed like it was supposed to be—easy.

Once I was back at college in the fall I returned to my "party lifestyle." I had a new roommate that year, but he only lasted a month before getting homesick and moving back home. Now I had my own place, my own space where I could do whatever I wanted. I spent a lot of time working out and perfecting different parts of my game. I knew this was my last chance to land a spot at the college of my dreams, the University of Akron. I wanted to play there desperately because it was close to home and I could go and play in front of my family and friends. Our team had a great season that year. We set the school record for most wins in a season and won multiple tournament games. At the end of the season I averaged twelve points a game, was named most outstanding defensive player, and selected to the all-conference team. I was glad to have accomplished all of this but I was still unsure of where I was going to go next. My coach reached out to the University of Akron to see if they would be interested in having me join their team for the 2000–01 basketball season. We'll come back to this a little later.

Chapter Three

WHIP IT GOOD!

In order to clear my head and gain some clarity on my future, I decided to take a trip to Myrtle Beach. This is where I went when I needed to start over. I was really looking forward to this trip because I was going with my friends from high school. I needed this trip. I needed to recharge and focus on what I was going to do next. The four of us hit the warm South Carolina beach and went wild. I decided the best way to forget about all the bad things I was going through was to get drunk (I mean really drunk) and find myself some female companionship. It did not take long before we achieved our goal. The second evening at our sunny paradise, I was consuming massive amounts of alcohol and decided to explore Ocean Boulevard searching for action. As I was wandering aimlessly around the crowded highway, I spotted a jeep full of beautiful girls. Don't ask me why, but I felt this strange urge to jump into a moving vehicle with these women I had never met before. As I emerged from the floor of the backseat, I found myself sitting next to a young Southern belle from Bristol, TN. I threw out the best pick-up line I could think of at the time, "Hey, I've decided you are going to be my girlfriend for the week." I know it sounds lame, but it actually worked.

By about day four of our summer extravaganza, I was looking for a way to accelerate our already out-of-control vacation. We ran into some guys we knew from high school. They were staying a few hotels down from us. As I walked into their hotel, I wasn't sure what was going on. All I know was I saw a handful of empty balloons and a bunch of extremely intoxicated high school seniors staring at the walls of a cheap motel room. It became clear to me that these men had been doing drugs for the last few days. Now I had been around drugs before: in fact, I had been known to smoke a little cannabis every once in a while, but this was entirely different. Turns out they were doing whip-its. To the best of my knowledge, doing a whip-it consisted of filling up a balloon with some type of gas and then ingesting it back into one's lungs. As I was sitting around the room, one of the impaired young men asked me if I wanted to take a turn. I don't know what it is about being in your early twenties, but youth causes some severe lapses in judgment. "Sure—why not?" I replied. Now, mind you, I had no idea what this was and had no clue what I was actually breathing into my lungs (sounds real smart, huh). After my second or third turn, we decided it was time to move on, time to look for our next high.

I don't remember a lot of what happened those last few days of the trip but I know something was going on inside of me. I had been exposed to a new way of living and I liked it. I had gone from what I thought was just innocent drinking and plunged head first into the world of addiction. Now just to clarify: addiction is not just limited to drugs and alcohol—you can become addicted to many things in this world. On top of the occasional drug and alcohol abuse, I found myself addicted to lying, fighting, and women. My life was now officially a train wreck. I was spiraling out of control and I saw no end in sight.

At the end of my eventful visit to the Palmetto State, I was really feeling lost. I wasn't sure where I would be living next year. I was partying HARD with my friends. Worst of all my girlfriend broke up with me. I was lost and hurting. I was searching for something to help me escape this nightmare. One rainy afternoon I drove by the Army

Infirmary and noticed a sign that says, "Do you think you're tough? Come find out how tough you really are at the Tough Man Contest!" Now this wasn't really an actual "Tough Man Competition," it was a knockoff version called "Meanest Man!" It was the same idea: grab a bunch of blokes off the street who think they can box and are crazy enough to step into a ring and let them beat the living daylights out off each other for three rounds. Now, I had just gotten into a fight a few months ago and won that one, so I thought to myself, *What the heck, sign me up!* I didn't know this at the time, but actual boxing is much different from everyday street fight. In boxing you need speed, endurance, and technique—as well as some sort of game plan to pummel your opponent into submission. Instead, as soon as I got into the ring and heard the first round bell, I started swinging as hard and fast as I could. I'm not sure if I actually made any contact with my opponent, but my ring coach seemed to be impressed by my performance. Before the third round he had given me a pep talk proclaiming, "One more round," just "one more round! I was exhausted and could barely move. My gloves felt like I was swinging 100-pound cinder blocks. I went at him with everything I had determined to knock him out. One more thing you should know about boxing before you step into the ring is to make sure to protect your jaw. Well, I didn't and he connected with a crushing right blow that sent my lifeless body to the floor. Next thing I know I'm sitting in the back of an ambulance with all the rest of the losers. I later found out that my opponent was some kind of boxing champion. He had won five of these competitions in the last few years. This event marked the end of my boxing career; "Tough Man"—not so much!

Chapter Four

AM I HEARING VOICES?

D o you remember that movie where that creepy little boy can see dead people? I remember the first time I watched that movie I was completely terrified. The thought of someone, especially a young person having communication with something not human, was really disturbing to me. While I was in my early twenties, I felt like that little boy. Something was going on inside of my body that I could not explain. It was so terrifying to me that it affected my life and held me captive for years. I am not sure when I started hearing them, but I remember having these *thoughts* and hearing strange *voices* urging me to do and say terrible things to people. At twenty-one years old I had never really read the Bible before, but I do remember hearing stories about people having demons attached to them. Was this what was happening to me?

Matthew 8:28–34: When He arrived at the other side in the region of Gadarenes, two demon-possessed men coming from the tombs met Him. They were so violent that no one could pass that way. "What do you want with us, Son of God?" they shouted. "Have you come here to torture us before the appointed time?"

Some distance from them a large herd of pigs was feeding. The demons begged Jesus, "If you drive us out, send us into the herd of pigs."

He said to them, "Go!" So they came out and went into the pigs, and the whole herd rushed down the step bank into the lake and died in the water. Those tending the pigs ran off, went into the town and reported all this, including what happened to the demon-possessed men. Then the whole town went out to meet Jesus. And when the saw Him, they pleaded with Him to leave their region.

What the heck, demons possessing people and making them do violent things and then jumping into a herd of pigs? This sounds more like a horror movie than real life. This Bible nonsense was way too bizarre for me to accept. There had to be a better explanation; maybe it was all the drugs and alcohol I had in my system (the mushrooms and whipits must be frying my brain). Yeah, that must be it! I just need a little time to detox, a little rest and relaxation and then I will be cool. It's funny what you can talk yourself into believing. Human beings are experts at trying to rationalize every minor or major event that happens in our lives. These voices weren't going away and unlike the story in Matthew, I had no herd of pigs to try and send them into.

I remember very vividly of going through a restaurant drive-thru in Urbana, Ohio. As we started to order our food, I became extremely anxious and paranoid. I remember having these terrible thoughts about hurting the workers inside the restaurant. All I could do to calm down the voices was to put my hand over my face and not look at anyone. As I pulled up to receive my order, I was in full-out panic mode. I believed if I let myself have any contact with the workers something bad would happen to them. Once I was taking someone home from practice after dark. I started to have these strange thoughts and anxieties that I had done something bad to this person. As soon as I got back to my house I called him just to make sure he was okay. This became a regular occurrence in my life. Anytime I was in a public place and people were around, I would start to experience this agonizing torture. Nothing I would do could stop them. It was almost as though whatever these things were, they were angry and they were determined to make my life a living nightmare.

I didn't tell many people about this because I was scared of two things: **first**, how they would treat me. I didn't want people to think I was crazy or scary and stop talking to me. I put on a good front: I only ever told one person about this, my ex-girlfriend. We went out to eat and I remember being so nervous, but I had to tell someone. The torture was eating away at me and I needed an advocate, someone to help get me through the pain. She was very understanding and helped me get my emotions under control. I am so grateful for that conversation. **Second**, I was scared what they might say. I did not want to hear someone say I needed to be in a mental hospital or I needed to be on medicine. So I just kept on living in sin, living in a darkness where no light could shine through. I typically would only encounter these voices every once in a while, but the more I was living this sinful lifestyle the more frequently the thoughts would creep into my head.

Chapter Five

LIFE AFTER EDISON

A fter my two years at Edison, I had to give up my apartment and move back home with my mom and dad. To say this was a bit of an adjustment was an understatement. At school I had no curfew, no restrictions, and no rules! Now I had to tell someone where I was going and what time I was coming home—although my parents were really cool about accountability, I still hated "checking in" (especially at 1:00 AM when you've had one too many whiskey and sodas.) But there were a lot of perks about moving back home. There was always an amazing meal at dinner. This was awesome because at school there were many days I was eating gas station food for lunch, continuously racking up the balance on the gas card they gave me for "emergency use only." It's also nice to have a washer and dryer that you don't have to spend $10 in quarters just to use. And Mom usually stepped up and tackled the huge mountain of laundry I had accumulated in one week's time (moms always know how to do your laundry just right.) Living at home was a great way to save money too. No more paying cable bill. No more paying rent to an angry landlord you keep ticking off with those "loud parties." Yes, living at home is a great way to save money—problem was I didn't have any to save.

Being twenty-one years old and not having any money is a real problem. There were times in my early twenties that I would have to ask my mom for some funds. Probably the most humiliating times were when I had a date and I had to ask my parents to "float me a twenty" to get me through the night. I remember taking a girl out around Halloween time. She was gorgeous and lived in a massive house in the suburbs of Cleveland. I don't remember her name, but I do remember she had a bunch of horses. In fact her family owned some western shop in town. This family had money, and lots of it. One evening I arrived at her house for our date. I planned on taking her to a Haunted House and dinner. Things were going really well until it was time to pay. I was on my "limited budget," care of Mommy and Daddy when I hear the worker say, "That will be $22." Now I had a big problem: I only had $20 and we hadn't even been to dinner yet. Determined not to look like a "cheapskate," I had to come up with a plan quickly. I got it, I thought to myself, I will say I left the money in my car and hopefully she will feel bad and just pay the guy herself (I was a real creep!) My plan was perfectly executed: by the time I got back from my car and into the line, she had already paid for the both of us. I have to say this was a rare occurrence. Most of my plans never turned out this well.

A few months later I landed my first real job. A friend of mine worked part time at a drive-thru liquor store about 30 minutes from my house. She told me they needed some help and asked me if I would be interested. I didn't have an extensive employment background; most every job I had I quit after a few months. I'm not really sure how I landed this job, but I suspect it was because I didn't live in that town and would be less likely to give away free beer and cigarettes to the local teenagers. My job duties were pretty simple: when a car pulled up, I got them what they needed and then took their money. I got to be pretty good recognizing the "repeat" customers; I would see their car coming and have their order ready for them—most of the time it was a dozen beers and a pack of cigarettes, the hard pack! I learned a lot from that job, some good but mostly BAD!

The people who worked with me were all very nice and always willing to help me. It didn't matter how much I screwed up, they were always willing to give me another chance. One of my biggest struggles was getting my cash register drawer to come out exactly right. I could never do it; I was always a few cents off. I remember one night one of my coworkers was counting her drawer in our break room. I walked by the open door and peeked in. I noticed this white power lying on the table and heard a voice say, "You want to try some?" Now in my short twenty-one years on this earth I felt like I had seen it all, like nothing could faze me or throw me off. As I searched for the words to respond back to this woman, I felt myself getting extremely nervous. This was my first time ever seeing cocaine, and I was really curious and a little tempted to try this drug out. I searched for just the right thing to say and out of my mouth I uttered "No I'm good, but thanks anyway."

I've made some really stupid decisions in my life, but thinking back years later, this was probably one of the best decisions I have ever made. I don't know why I said no to this opportunity when I said yes to most of the other ones in my life. I guess something inside of me knew if I crossed over into the world of cocaine, there would be no going back.

I continued to work at the drive thru for another few months. I also began taking some classes at the University of Akron. I liked being back at school because it helped me return to some type of "normal" schedule. I was working out three days a week, playing in as many open gyms and recreational basketball leagues as I could find, and was taking twelve credit hours at the college.

One afternoon coming home from class, I saw a handwritten phone message my brother had left for me. I still remember the feeling I got when my mind actually pieced the words together on that small yellow post-it-note lying on our kitchen table. The note was the message I had been waiting for my entire basketball career. My dream college (The University of Akron) called and wanted to meet with me in regards to joining their men's basketball team. I couldn't believe it—I took a deep breath, grabbed the phone, and slowly dialed the number to the athletic office. I got a hold of the coach's secretary and made an appointment to meet with the head coach. This was it, everything I had worked so hard for was about to come true. I could not contain my excitement, I called the first person I could think of, my mom!

The day of my appointment was all a blur. I remember searching for a parking space and making my way into the Field House in search of the coaches' office. I went down a long hallway lined with famous Akron alumni who have excelled at some type of sport. I remember it being difficult to actually muster the courage to walk into the office. I think I walked back and forth about three times before I actually entered the office. After I walked in, I was greeted by the secretary and could see into the assistant coach's office. This was it I couldn't screw this up—I needed to make a good impression and convince this guy he needed me on his team. After a few minutes the head coach emerged from his office and greeted me with a handshake. I can still remember how tall he was and the big smile across his face. We sat down and talked for a while; he asked me questions like "You look like you put some weight on, have you been lifting?" "Yes," I replied! Then he asked me, "Can you still jump as high as you used to?" "Yes, I can," I replied confidently. After a few minutes of talking, his son came into the office and sat down to join the conversation. He was also a member of the basketball team. The last time I saw this guy he was just a skinny little child, now he was a 6-foot 6 grown man. We talked for a little while longer about what I have been doing the last couple years. Finally when it was about time for me to leave, I heard the words I have been longing to hear. "Brian, I know you can play—why don't you join our basketball team? You can start practicing with us immediately." I couldn't believe it—these are the words that I had been aching to hear for some many years. My dream was finally coming true.

After a few minutes of pure joy, I was brought back down to reality. Remember that old college basketball regulations and rules? Well, they came back to bite me in the "You know what again." Apparently, there are rules about transferring from a junior college to a Division 1 school. If you don't graduate with an associate's degree from your institution, you have to sit out one full calendar year. I guess my class load at Edison full of courses like "Basketball Officiating," "Volleyball," and "History of Rock & Roll" doesn't carry much weight when it comes to actually graduating from an academic institution. So I was not eligible to play in the 1999–00 season.

After receiving that devastating news, I decided to put it behind me and thought I was just going to work and get myself ready for the next season. And although I was disappointed I did have one thing to look forward to that year, my twenty-first birthday. On December 29, 2000, I was finally legal to drink in the State of Ohio. No more fake IDs. No more sneaking into bars. No more hiding alcohol from my parents—I was twenty-one and ready to celebrate. On my birthday my friends took me out to a country bar called the "Saloon." This place was exactly like it sounds, a bunch of country music, cowboys, and girls. I was going "hard" that night. Shots, dollar beers, you name it I would drink it. As we were leaving, I decided to continue the party out into the parking lot. Since it was winter time and we had a few inches of snow on the ground, I thought it might be funny to start making snow balls and pelting cars as they were exiting the parking lot (I know I'm an idiot!). I remember one car full of guys who just so happened to have their window rolled down. I made the perfect snowball; it was just the right mixture of snow, ice, and a little touch of frozen mud. I had the car in my sights, I wound up and let loose, and … it was a perfect strike! I threw that snowball right through the window (I couldn't have done that again if I had ten chances). Well, this group of cowboys didn't really care for my choice of drunken, birthday fun. Next thing I know six guys jumped out of the car and were looking for a fight. Consuming massive amounts of alcohol really makes you do some stupid things. Add your group of friends to the mix and all of a sudden you feel invincible (darn liquid courage.) Luckily for me this was not the first altercation my friends and I had gotten ourselves into. Next thing I knew fists were flying, bodies were lying on the ground, and security guards and police were everywhere. This little "misunderstanding" lasted only a few minutes and then it was over as quickly as it started. You know what I love about guys? They get over things fast.... After the fight was over, I remember having my arm around and laughing with this man who minutes later was trying to rearrange my face with his boot.

So this was my life: drinking, drugs, women, and basketball. It was a constant cycle of events that played itself out over and over almost every day of my life. Something needed to change or I was going to end up in jail or killing myself. I remember thinking, *There has to be more than this.* I felt this huge hole in my soul, like I was only half a person. I needed a change and it needed to happen now!

Growing up I was never really a religious person. My parents would take each of us kids to church on Sunday mornings and maybe I would attend a random youth group meeting. I did do some occasional praying, but it was usually relegated to only on those occasions where I needed to get out of trouble ("Dear God, please don't let me get arrested tonight, I promise I will go to church on Sunday!"). I didn't know Jesus or what it meant to be one of His followers, but I did know He was famous for helping people out from time to time.

One evening I was lying in my bed and for whatever reason I started talking to God. It wasn't a long conversation, but I told Him I couldn't even stand to look at myself anymore and I really needed His help. I told God that night that I was "desperate" and gave Him permission to change my life by "any means necessary!" I've done a lot of dangerous things in my life, but praying that prayer to Jesus on that dark night was probably the most dangerous thing I had ever done in my life. I learned that night if you pray those type of prayers (I call them **dangerous prayers**), you better be ready for Him to show up. Maybe in ways you never dreamed of. That's what happened to me. God answered my prayer, but not in the way I had expected He would!

Matthew 7:7–8: "Ask and it will be given to you; seek and you will find; knock and the door will be opened to you. For everyone who asks receives; he who seeks finds; and to him who knocks, the door will be opened."

Chapter Six

THE NIGHT IT ALL CHANGED

I n May of that year, my brother helped me get a job with one of his friends as a concrete laborer. This was a great job for me: it was physical, so that helped me stay in good basketball shape, plus the pay was good, so I always had money in my pocket. I had never really done any type of construction work before, so I had to learn a lot. Most of what my job entailed was to push the fresh concrete around after it came off the truck. I put on these yellow rubber boots and trudged my way through cement for eight hours a day. By the time I made it home, I was too tired to even go out with my friends. What I loved about that job was everyday was something new. I always had an opportunity to learn a new part of the concrete business. One of coolest jobs working with concrete is the "finisher." To be able to do this job you have to have some skill. Your main purpose as a finisher was to smooth out the quick drying cement before it got too hard to move. I only tried this once and I was not very good at it. I was way too slow and had no artistic ability! I was a hired hand, and my specialty was brute force: push and carry as much concrete as humanly possible by the end of the workday.

One Saturday afternoon my boss and I were finishing up a driveway. We poured the concrete the day before so we were back to do the cutting. After we had finished working for the day, we went out to grab some lunch at a local Irish Tavern. I had never been to this place before but since I am half Irish, it sounded pretty cool. As we sat down to order our food, we were joined by a couple more of our friends. One of the really interesting things about this restaurant is the atmosphere. They have fresh popcorn that is constantly being popped to enjoy alongside your meal. I also remember a little bar area that was stocked full of any liquor you could imagine. We all decided to sample a few beers while we were eating our lunch. After we finished eating, I decided I wanted to get everyone at the table a shot. Now, I should have known this was going to end badly when I decided to start doing shots of liquor at 12:00 in the afternoon. I walked up over to the bartender and hollered out my order. "Give me four shots of *something hard!*" If you have never consumed a shot of Firewater, I assure you it tastes just like it sounds. The bartender gave us our drinks and we toasted together for a great day!

After we finished eating our lunch, the next stop was a place near my house. This establishment was an exotic dancer bar (is that the politically correct term for it?). Now, I have been in some hole in the wall, downright nasty clubs before, but this place was different, a light bit more upscale. As soon as you walk into the door it feels like another world. For a twenty-one-year-old immature kid, this place was like heaven. I look to my left and saw the pool tables. Straight ahead was the bar area. To my right—yep, you guessed it, the girls. A whole bunch of half-naked females, dancing around for drunken men who are just naive enough to think they actually have a chance to take one of them home. After "enjoying the view" for a few moments, I did what I always do when I'm at one of these establishments—I pushed my way to the bar. One of the perks of coming to this place was that we knew the bartenders. He asked me what I wanted to drink and I told him, "Give me four shots!" He asked me what kind of shots I wanted. After consuming multiple drinks of hard liquor, I thought it was time for a change. So I told him to make us something strong! After a few minutes had passed, the bartender set our drinks down and said "Here's four shots of swimmer on acid. Enjoy!" At that point a red flag should have jumped out at me: anytime you are consuming an alcoholic beverage with word "acid" attached to it, you better proceed with extreme caution. I am not exactly sure how many of these drinks I actually had, but I must have had quite a few because my memory started to get a little fuzzy at this point.

Now that the drinks were taken care of, it was time to turn my attention to more important matters—the dancers. I made my way to the back of the room and sat down at the table. Located at the other side of the bar was a small dance floor where the ladies would showcase their talents. I decided it was better for me to sit in the back, mostly because I didn't have any money and didn't want to be that creepy guy with no money who just stares at the girls all night. After watching a few dancers take the stage, one of the ladies caught my eye. She was beautiful; she definitely didn't look like any dancer I had ever seen. She looked like she belonged on the cover of a magazine, not some "dancer bar" on the south side of Canton. I decided I was going to get her to notice me. I ordered a few drinks and asked her to sit down with us. We were having a great conversation. I threw every line I had at her. I told her I wanted to take her out sometime. To my amazement she said okay and actually gave me her number. I know the logical part of my brain should have thought, *Dude, this girl is a dancer; she probably gives a fake number to all the guys.* I didn't care—I took her number, put it in my pocket, and proceeded to enjoy my evening.

It was about 8:00 PM and we decided it was time to leave. I said goodbye to my new dancer friend and assured her I would "give her a call." I remember stepping outside onto wet pavement. It must have rained at some point when we were inside. I didn't mind, at this point I welcomed a little cool, fresh air. Since I was obviously in no condition to drive, I jumped into my buddy's vehicle and prepared for the 15-minute ride home. As we pulled out of the parking lot, it must have been hot because I rolled down the window of the soft top jeep. It started to sprinkle. The raindrops slowly peppered the windshield as we got onto the entrance ramp heading north on Interstate 77. This is one of the last memories I have of that night, and it is one of the last memories I have of my old life!

As we made our way back home, the rain started to pick up. The pavement was now full of puddles of water all across the expressway. In an instant, the driver of our vehicle lost control. We were spinning out of control and slammed into the side of a guardrail. Upon impact I was ejected out of the side passenger window 50 feet down a hill and landed in a ditch. (Obviously I wasn't wearing my seatbelt—I always thought I was too cool for them—not so cool now!) My first thought after I hit the ground was to run. So I picked my battered and bruised body up of the ground and tried to sprint back up the hill. I only made it a couple steps before I collapsed back down to the ground. I tried to get back but couldn't. All I could do was just stare up at the sky and wonder what was going on. I must have passed out for a few minutes because I don't really remember what happened next.

Have you ever had one of those experiences in your life where something happened that was so amazing, so miraculous, so incredible that you knew it had to be from God? The next 10 minutes of my life were one of those experiences. As I lay on that cold, wet grass floating in and out of consciousness, I started to hear voices (and not the voices I was talking about earlier). These were calming voices telling me that everything was going to be okay, telling me they would take care of me. I opened my eyes and saw women sitting behind me, one of them with her hands clasped around my neck telling me "not to move." I wondered who these women were and what they were doing to me. It turned out these weren't just ordinary women, they were a car full of nurses (or I like to call them, my car full of angels) headed to their job at the local hospital just a few miles from the accident. I don't know who these women were or where they came from, but I'm pretty sure they helped save my life. It was more than pure luck that these nurses were driving down the exact road at the exact time I needed them. It was more than luck that these nurses were able to locate my body after it was thrown 50 feet down a hill and into a ditch. It was more than luck—it was God!

Chapter Seven

AT THE HOSPITAL

Once an emergency crew arrived at the scene, they secured my neck and loaded me into the ambulance. It wasn't a long ride to the hospital but it felt like it took forever. The EMS workers kept asking me questions and the only words I could utter were "I don't want to die!" The workers did a great job reassuring me I was going to make it, but I knew something was wrong, really wrong.

I wasn't in a lot of pain but everything felt numb (kind of like when your foot falls asleep from sitting on it too long.) I felt this way from my chest all the way to my feet. Everyone kept asking me if I could move my legs—I tried and tried but they wouldn't budge, not even an inch. I tried again, nothing. According to the medical reports, I continued to tell everyone my legs were fine and that I was just tired. The amazing thing about this accident is other than the fact that I couldn't move my legs or parts of my arms, I didn't have a scratch on me (except for the bleeding that was coming out of my ears, but I guess that is consistent with a traumatic accident?) On the outside, everything looked completely normal, but internally my body was in a fight—a fight to stay alive!

After arriving at Aultman Hospital, I was immediately admitted to the ICU. The Intensive Care Unit was a strange place. It was extremely loud. People were always yelling and the nurses kept asking me the same questions. I remember loud beeping noises that made sleeping nearly impossible. The medical staff gave me a complete physical examination. After determining my vitals were stable, the staff wrote this statement in my medical chart:

> **Physical Examination:** A *healthy, well-nourished, 21-year old male who looks like his chronological age. He is in no acute distress. Vital signs are stable. Neurological examination reveals he is awake, alert and appropriately oriented. He dozes off to sleep consistent to it being 1 o'clock in the morning and his level of alcohol intoxication (.206). His visual fields are full. Extraocular muscles are intact. Facial strength is symmetric. He has virtually normal deltoid and biceps strength bilaterally. He gives good effort with these muscles. However, he is unable to move his triceps or grasp intrinsic muscles at all bilaterally. He is unable to move his legs or feet at all. He does have intact sensation throughout his upper extremities and he is able to detect which leg I am touching without error although he says the farther I go down his leg the less feel he has. His rectal tone is flaccid and he is unable to contract my finger."*

All of this is just fancy doctor-speak for "You are really messed up and we have no idea how bad."

I was sent down to radiology to have a complete MRI and CAT scan performed. At this point I lost complete track of all time. I couldn't tell you what time it was, what day it was, and I probably would have screwed up the year. Life as I knew it had just stopped. Nothing made any sense. People kept coming into my room and poking me with different objects asking me if I could feel it. I thought to myself, *I don't care how far you shove that pin into my leg, I can't feel it!* I found myself surrounded by people but all alone. The medical staff kept asking me where my parents were, but I would only tell them, "I said it's okay—they're on vacation. We don't need to bother them right now. I will call them on Monday." They did their best to try and convince me of the urgency of the situation, but I refused to believe this nightmare was happening (hence the .206 BAC.) Finally I broke down and told them, "They are at the Campground." That really wasn't helpful information because there are hundreds of campsites at this campground. Eventually they got a hold of the Ranger Station who, in turn, tracked down my parents. I often wonder what my parents' reaction was when they heard this news. I'm sure they had to be completely shocked and terrified. Since neither of my parents was in any state (complete shock) to drive to the hospital, one of their friends from the campground made the 45-minute drive for them. I can only imagine what was going through their minds as they had to sit and wonder what was going on with their son and was he going to be okay. I really hate myself for putting my family through this!

After arriving at the hospital, my parents were taken into this little conference room and waited for the doctor to come in and tell them what was going on. I can only imagine the terror wrecking my mother's brain. I can see the pain and agony welling up in her tear-filled eyes. This was her little boy and she could do nothing to help him. And my dad, what was going through his mind? This is the man who taught me to throw a baseball, catch a fish, and drive a car. This is the man who drove 3 ½ hours to help me in college when my car broke down. He would have done anything to help me, anything to keep me safe—but he was helpless now. I was the IDIOT who caused this mess and there was only one person who could help me now—God.

This is the point of my story that still haunts my dreams. To know that I put my family through the next ten minutes of living hell is almost too much for me to take. After what must have felt like an eternity, the doctor finally came in and delivered the news. "Your son was involved in a terrible *motor vehicle accident* and was hurt badly.

He was thrown from the vehicle and sustained extensive damage to his spinal cord. At this moment we are not sure of prognosis, but just in case you will want to contact your local funeral home to start the process of making arrangements. If by some miracle your son makes it through the night, he will need major surgery to repair the damage to his spinal cord. Brian will most likely not recover neurologic function and will probably spend the rest of his life in a wheelchair." The doctor said he wanted to wait to discuss this with me because at the moment I was unable to comprehend what we would be discussing.

This was the "danger zone" time of my accident. No one was really sure if I was going to live or die. I wish I could say I had some miraculous event like that little boy who died and went to Heaven and got to see all his family and got all those cool revelations from God. Nope, that didn't happen to me. In fact, if I died, I would have probably got the personalized tour of hell instead.

Sometime later after I sobered up, the doctor came into my room along with my parents. I was relieved to see my family but completely ashamed of my actions. Next the doctor told me what happened to me. He said, "Brian, you broke your neck and will probably never walk again!" This is not exactly what I had in mind when I asked God to make a change in my life. He proceeded to tell me that I had "burst" my C5 vertebrae and I was paralyzed from the neck down. I was diagnosed with quadriplegia. With this type of injury level, 90 percent of people never regain the ability to walk. We would need to perform surgery on Monday morning. That two-minute conversation seemed to destroy every single dream or goal I set for my life. I would never play basketball again. I would never get married. I would never have any children. Now I know I had done some bad things in my life, but I didn't deserve this, did I?

I heard everything the doctor was saying but I refused to believe any of it. I still held on to hope that the next day I would wake up and this would all be a terrible nightmare. After the doctor had finished his little pep talk, I noticed a few of my friends and family starting to gather around the waiting room area. One by one they each came into my room and hugged me and told me how much they loved me. I was so grateful for each and every visitor. Before I knew it the entire ICU was packed full of people coming in to check on me. I guess it got so full that the nurses had to start kicking people out of the hallway. These people were amazing and I love each and every one of them. One of my fondest memories was when one of my best friends curled up in bed with me and just laid with me for a while. They kept coming in giving me support, telling me that "I could beat this." "I could be in that 10 percent and walk again." They all mean so much to me and I am so blessed to have them in my life. I didn't deserve that type of love. I didn't deserve that type of response. I acted selfish, careless, and ungrateful! I put innocent lives in danger. I may not have been the one driving the car but I was equally responsible.

Monday morning came for my surgery. The surgeon told me he was going to make a small incision in the front of my neck so he could get to my spinal cord. He said the surgery was going to be a corpectomy of C5 and a fusion from C4–C6. Next, they would take a piece of my hip bone and graft it to my spinal column. Then he would drill four holes into the vertebrae and attach them with four screws. The purpose was to clean out all the fragmented broken vertebrae that could potentially damage the spinal cord. My spinal fracture was considered an "incomplete injury" because the spinal cord was bruised and not severed. I developed a hematoma on the site of the break that was preventing normal "neurological activity." The hope of the surgery was to stabilize the neck and hope that enough of the bruising and swelling went down that I may get some motor function back.

After the surgery, they fitted me the most uncomfortable neck brace ever made. I was told to wear this thing for three months. I remember being completely dependent on other people to take care of all my basic needs. Because I had paralysis in my arms, I could not reach high enough to shave this "mountain man" beard that was starting to take over my face. My dad would do his best to shave what he could without moving my head and getting shaving cream down the side of my brace. I guess I shouldn't complain because some spinal cord patients have to wear halos. Those are big metal contraptions that hold your neck in place with two screws drilled into your forehead. My neck brace had the type of fabric much like what they use for people who tear their ACL. It was itchy and smelly and I wanted that thing off as soon as possible.

Besides the neck brace, I had to adapt to an entirely new way of living. The simple things in life like brushing my teeth, combing my hair, and even getting myself dressed had come to an end. It's funny how much of the little stuff in life I took for granted. I remember seeing people in wheelchairs when I was younger and thinking to myself how much that would suck. In high school when one of my friends was paralyzed in an accident, I even made the ignorant statement of "If I was ever paralyzed and in a wheelchair, I would definitely kill myself!" It's funny how that statement came full circle. The ironic part of it was even if I wanted to hurt myself, I couldn't do it—I would have had to ask someone else for help: *Um, Nurse Kelly, I'm feeling really depressed today—would you mind pushing my wheelchair out in front of the moving truck, please? Thanks, I appreciate the help!*

This was my new life and everyone on my medical team was telling me to get used to it. *This is your new life. Well, I don't want this life. I hate this life. I'm ready to wake up from this horrible nightmare.* None of this was making sense. Where was this God that was supposed to help people? I did my part, right? I prayed—I asked God to make me a better person. Instead I'm sitting in a hospital bed paralyzed from the neck down. If this was God's sense of humor, I was not laughing. I think it was at this time that I shut any religious part of my brain down. I figured if God wasn't going to help me, I guess I had to try and do this all by myself (because that had worked so well for me in the past). So I reverted back to what came natural to me—athletics. I got myself into the mindset that I was going to beat this injury. I thought to myself, *I'm not going to let some doctor or nurse tell me what I can or cannot do. I'll show them. I will get back on my feet again, even if it kills me!* At this point in my recovery I didn't know a whole lot about spinal cord injuries. Working hard, having great determination, and refusing to give up are all important in regaining function, but in the end most of spinal cord injury recoveries are by pure luck (and of course, God). I've seen people with quadriplegia work countless hours a day in the gym. Push their wheelchairs until their hands would bleed. Then go to bed hooked up to the latest SCI technology and they only regain a minimal amount of muscle control. Then on the other side, I have seen people who do nothing but lay in their beds and watch TV make full recoveries. It all comes down to level of injury and the amount of damage to the spinal cord. It isn't totally dependent on "hard work." But I didn't know that and I was too hardheaded to listen to people who were just trying to prepare me for the future.

I spent two more weeks in the Intensive Care Unit at Aultman Hospital. I was completely confined to my bed. People continued to stop by on a daily basis to check on my progress. I loved the conversations I had with them. It was these little random acts of kindness that got me through those dark days. One of my favorite "visitor stories" took place a few days after I was transferred out of the ICU and up to a regular room. A few of my basketball friends stopped by to say hello. These guys were tall, really tall, and they took up a lot of space in my tiny little hospital room. After they left the nurses were all excited. They couldn't believe the size of these men. I think they thought LeBron James and Michael Jordan had just stopped by to see me. Although it was great to see my old friends, it made me really miss my basketball days.

One of the things I learned from this accident was that in order to maximize your opportunity for muscle return, the doctors wanted me to find an in-patient rehabilitation institution as quickly as possible so I could begin therapy. This was a difficult decision for my family and we had no I idea how to go through it. We tried to do as much investigating as possible, but we really only had two options that were close to our home. There was a facility in Akron and one in Cleveland. We decided to go with MetroHealth Medical Center in Cleveland, Ohio. One of our family friends who had a similar injury as mine had gone through therapy there and seemed to have a good experience. Now that we had finalized that decision, we had to make sure I was physically capable of being moved from the hospital. Because I had spent so much time lying on my back, I developed two red and inflamed "bed sores" on the back of my heels. Bed sores are a big hazard for patients with spinal cord injuries because they can become infected and cause big problems. To help get the sores to heal and prevent them from getting any worse, I was fitted with two extremely uncomfortable and really ugly-looking boots (I call them my moon boots). It was also important that before I was moved anywhere, I could tolerate being able to sit for an extended period of time. Since I had spent so much time in bed, my body had to slowly acclimate to being tolerant of a sitting position (it's kind of like those individuals who get altitude sickness from climbing those huge mountains—more on that to come).

My first session of physical therapy was definitely a memorable one. As I was lying in bed waiting for it to begin, I was playing one of my favorite "time passing" activities—count the number of ceiling tiles. I got to be pretty good at it. Something tells me I'm not the only quadriplegic who has played this exciting game! Then two women appeared in my room and introduced themselves to me. They told me they were my therapists and today they were going to put me in a chair that was sitting on the left side of my room. I wasn't sure how these two little women were going to get my paralyzed self out of bed and into that chair. They wasted no time: one therapist took my right side and sure enough the other took my left. They counted out loud, "1, 2, 3—lift!" and they threw my 200-pound body into the chair with relative ease. This was when I first realized how strong an in-patient physical therapist needed to be. Once they got me into the chair, I began to get really dizzy. After about 15 seconds I felt like I was going to puke. Then I slowly started to shrink into the chair and felt myself falling towards the floor. The therapists grabbed a hold of me, picked me up, and placed me back into my bed. I thought to myself, *That was it, 15 seconds—man, I'm in big trouble!*

The day had finally come for me to be transported from Aultman Hospital to my rehab facility, Cleveland Metro Health Medical Center. I was scared and had no idea what to expect. Because the ride to Cleveland was about 50 miles and the fact that I was still in such fragile condition, I had to be transported by ambulance. The only part of that ride that I still remember is how bumpy it was. Every time we hit a pothole, I felt like I was going to hit the roof of the ambulance. My body was so tensed up and I was worried one of the screws in my neck was going to come loose. After what seemed like a two-hour ride, we finally arrived at the facility. I remember being taken out of the back of the ambulance and looking up and seeing the big emergency sign on the wall. At this point I was all by myself. My parents drove separately and were going to meet us here. There was a different feeling about this place. MetroHealth is a level 1 trauma center and deals with everything from heart attacks to gunshots. I can't really describe it, but I could almost feel the despair and sadness illuminating through the air. There were people everywhere, and everybody looked sad or upset. As my bed was pushed further and further into the hospital, it occurred to me how real this was. We got to a set of elevators and made our way up to floor number seven. As I made my way down the hallway, I started to see people in wheelchairs. Some of them were smiling, some were not. I could feel them all looking at me trying to figure out my story, trying to figure out who I was and where I came from. I remember the smell of that floor—it was terrible! It smelled like a mixture of feces and urine. I was then wheeled into my room. My room was right next to the nurses' station because I still had multiple health concerns and needed to be monitored closely. The attendants then moved me from the backboard onto my bed. After that they left me. I was lying on the bed with no sheets or blankets and I was so cold—shivering in fact. I needed my parents. I didn't care if I was a twenty-one-year-old man, I wanted my mom. After what seemed like forever, my parents finally made it to my room. When they found me, I burst into tears. I think this was the first time since my accident that I actually cried. I pleaded with my parents to take me home; "I couldn't do this," I said. My father reassured me, "Just give it a few days. If you don't like it, I will take you home." My dad was awesome! He knew there was no way he was taking me home from that hospital, but at that time it was exactly the words that I needed to hear. It was those simple loving words that carried me through the *scariest time of my life.*

I know God was doing His thing through this entire experience, but what He did next was nothing short of "life changing!" I believe God knew that in order for me to be able to survive in this crazy environment I needed help, and not help from an "able-bodied person." I needed help from somebody going through the exact same thing as I was—someone who I could heal with. Enter Joe Harper, aka "The Giggler." Joe was my new roommate and to say that we came from different "walks of life" would be an understatement of cosmic proportions. Joe was charismatic, humorous, outgoing, and welcoming. I was shy, reserved, arrogant, and scared. He was from Cleveland, an extremely bad section of Cleveland. I was from a little rural town where we still left our doors open at night. We were complete opposites, from totally different worlds, but God brought us together because I needed him and he needed me. And we were about to take MetroHealth by storm!

One of my favorite memories of Joe was when he used to rap for me in our room. Joe was an aspiring rap artist who went by the alias "The Giggler." He would always try to get me to "flow" with him, but I was way too shy. One afternoon Joe got a visitor; his name was

Proof—and he was a professional rapper from the group D12. I knew about Proof because he made records with one of my favorite artists of all time—Eminem.

They don't waste much time in rehab before they throw you into therapy. Every day was scheduled and it started early. My day started out with breakfast: if my parents were there they would have to help me eat; if not it would be one of the nurses. Then it was time to get dressed; this always seemed to be a chore. First they had to put on these "tights" to keep circulation moving through my legs, then they would sit me up and gently try and get me shirt to fit over my obnoxious-looking neck brace. After this came the fun part—trying to get on my underwear. Because it wasn't only the outside of my body that was paralyzed (i.e. my legs and arms), I had paralysis affecting some of my internal organs as well. One of the most affected areas was my bladder. I couldn't hold my urine like a normal person. So to correct this, I was fitted for an internal catheter. Oh, what I joy this contraption was! If you haven't ever had the pleasure of having one of these devices inserted into your body, let me give you a brief description.

A catheter is a rubber tube inserted into the bladder for the purpose of removing fluid. Sounds like fun, doesn't it? This is one of the times it worked in my favor to be a quad. I had no feeling from the chest down. So as the nurse was getting me dressed in the morning, he needed to make sure that my underwear and pants made it safely over the top of the catheter or else it would dislodge and I would have a bed full of "smelly pee." Yep, this was my new and exciting life at twenty-one years old!

After I had finished getting dressed, it was time to take my medicine. Since I had so many health issues that need to be managed, I took about 6,000 pills a day—exaggerating, of course. But there were a lot. I had no idea what I was taking. I just knew there was a constant flow of pills and injections that I needed to have in order to keep me alive. Once I threw down that last pill, it was time for therapy. I could do therapy—it reminded me a lot of my old basketball practices. We had four seasons of therapy throughout the day: two in the morning and another two in the afternoon. If it wasn't for these four hours a day, I don't think I would have made it. I used every ounce of strength and every available muscle to try and get myself better. Even after my session was over, I asked if I could stay longer to work out. I felt somewhat normal in that therapy room, like I had a chance.

My therapist, Deb, was amazing! From the moment she started working with me she always kept a positive attitude. When the world was telling me I couldn't do something, she convinced me I could. When the world was telling me to slow down, she hollered at me to speed up. I don't know where I would have ended up without her. I am eternally grateful that God placed her in my life to be MY therapist.

After working a few weeks with Deb, it was time for my family to make a decision. The medical staff was trying to get me to pick out my future means of transportation—a wheelchair. I remember the staff bringing in brochure after brochure of different styles and models of the latest and greatest wheelchairs. They tried their best to entice me with statements like "Look at this color, Brian, wouldn't it be cool to have a blue chair?" Or, "Man this chair is cool; you don't even have to push it, the thing moves by itself!" I typically responded to those comments with my true "jerk guy" type attitude. If I could have moved my arms, I would have probably thrown those brochures on the ground or worse, punched one of those nice young social workers in the face. I didn't want to hear it. I didn't want to think about it. It wasn't going to happen. I will not be going home in one of those stupid chairs!

Eventually I did have to face reality. I wasn't getting any better and I was sick of having to rely on people to take me everywhere I wanted to go. I was desperate for some type of independence. I gave in and agreed to at least try out a wheelchair. The first chair brought for me to try was one of those power chairs that you controlled with your hand. They are pretty cool, like you're playing an old game system without the really sweet graphics. Although this was the logical choice for me to use because I had barely any muscle in my arms, I refused it and asked them to bring me a manual chair that I could push with my own weak, girly arms. They weren't buying it—they were insistent that I use the power chair because I could not operate the manual one safely and, not to mention, I couldn't even move the dang thing! I fought them and demanded they bring me something I could push—if my legs weren't going to move, I was determined to strengthen what little muscles I had working in my arms. I think it was at this point that the nice people at MetroHealth realized they were going to have a real battle on their hands with me. I was extremely "hardheaded" and wasn't going to just go along with the normal protocol. This type of stubborn attitude may have seemed counterproductive at the time but, looking back, it was probably a big reason for my recovery.

A few days later after I finished my daily morning routine, my new wheels came rolling through the door. It was a strange feeling of terror, excitement, and a wee bit of anger. My therapist came in and sat me up at the edge of my bed. I was staring at this machine wondering how in the world I was going to get on it. I was then given this short piece of slippery wood that sort of resembled a paddle that my fifth grade principal used to use on all the bad kids. Next they took that piece of wood and shoved one side of it under my butt. Then they grabbed me by the shoulders and slid my limp and weak body from the bed into the chair. It was called a "transfer," and that was the first of hundreds of times I would do this over the next six months. Once I was into the chair, I felt very unstable. Because I didn't have any ab muscles, my body wanted to fall forward onto the cold hard floor. To correct this, I had a tight white elastic band wrapped around my torso and back of the chair. This kept me straight and upright. After I was situated properly, they grabbed one foot at a time and placed it into the proper footrest. I was almost ready to go; all I needed was a pair of gloves and I was about to tear this hospital apart. My therapist wheeled me out into the hallway and just left me. She told me to meet her in half an hour for my therapy session. Yes, this was it! Finally, a little freedom! I could go anywhere I wanted and nobody was going to stop me. I pulled my left arm up and gently placed it on the wheel. Then I did the same thing with my right arm. I took a few breaths and got myself pumped and ready to move. Here we go, "1, 2, and 3—" and I pushed that chair with every ounce of muscle my paralyzed body could muster. I didn't move. I tried it again, same result. What's going on here, this wasn't part of my master plan. After about 20 minutes had passed, I only managed to move a couple inches. At this point in time someone came and checked on me. "Not as easy as you thought, huh, Brian?" *Shut up—I got this, man!* I thought I just needed a little more practice; I just needed some time to adjust.

Meanwhile things were not looking so good in my recovery. The more days that passed with no movement in my legs, the less likely I would ever recover function with them. I also started to develop ailments that were common to a person with quadriplegia—phantom pain and muscles spasms. Phantom pain is a little difficult to explain. From what I remember even though my legs were paralyzed and couldn't move, I was still getting throbbing pain throughout them (this was weird because I was a quad and had no feeling). Muscle spasms were different. This annoying little medical condition was caused by nerves that go from my brain through my spinal cord getting all screwed up because of the injury to my neck. The result was a whole bunch of muscles randomly jumping or twitching for no reason. Apparently this was a good thing. My doctor said that the muscle movement was good for my paralyzed limbs because it would help prevent them from developing atrophy. I also was continuing to battle issues with my bowel and bladder. That catheter that I hated so much was doing its job but I had been at the facility for about ten days and still had yet to have a bowel movement. To help along with this process, my doctor decided it was time for me to have my very first enema (yea!!!). To me this was as about as inhumane as it gets. After the nurse inserted this medicine into my "booty region," they placed a bunch of towels on my bed and laid me on my side. Now I'm not a medical professional, but it seems to me there has got to be a better way of going about this process than having your patient literally lying in his own feces for an hour while the enema does its thing—but hey, what do I know?

So at about this time in my recovery I was about as low as you can get. After being manhandled by the nurses and having every part of your manhood and dignity stripped away, I was done with this paralyzed gig. I felt alone, angry, sad, and extremely depressed. I was done with this life and started to think maybe it wasn't worth living anymore. It was at this point that I got some help from an unexpected source. I turned to music as a way to escape this living hell I found myself trapped in. One day I was given a CD of Eminem entitled, *The Marshal Mathers LP*. It was as if this CD was written exclusively for me and everything I was going through. I know Eminem is a very controversial rap artist, but I will tell you one thing: listening to Eminem at this stage of my recovery helped save my life! There was just something about the anger and pain that was showing through the lyrics that I was connecting with. I remember putting on that CD, sitting in my chair, and staring out the window yearning for the day I could break out of this place and start living again.

I would listen to this album for hours and slowly I felt something starting to change inside of myself. Suddenly I felt like it was time I stopped feeling sorry for myself and started to live my life again (no matter how different my life looked right now!). I allowed myself to release all that anger and rage I had built up inside of me through the music. I lost myself inside the lyrics. Looking back at this crucial point in my life, I can honestly say that I came to Christ (in large part) because of Eminem and his music!

It's funny because up to this point I was really never talking to God. I didn't pray for Him to make me walk again. I didn't yell and scream and demand an answer from Him. I just totally ignored Him, I left God out of the most crucial and important time of my twenty-one years on earth. As humans we do this all the time. We think we got it all together. We think we can handle any situation. We think we don't need God. And that is exactly what I had been doing since my accident. So I started to pray. I prayed simple prayers. I asked God for small miracles that would help me make it through another day. This was when it all changed—this was when I started to understand the power of prayer.

"I have so much to do that I shall spend the first three hours in prayer!"

In the next few weeks I witnessed God start do amazing things with my recovery. During one of my countless examinations with my physicians, I was asked to try and move my toe. I had tried this many times before and was not able to do it. The doctor said, "Try and move your toe." I tried to remember what it actually felt like to move my toe. I flexed my foot with everything I had in me. I heard him say, "Did you see that?" Then I was told to do it again; this time I peeked up and watched my big toe move ever so slightly. I was ecstatic! I couldn't believe what I just saw—I was actually moving my toe! I did it a few more times before the little muscle I had working in my toe gave out. I was happy, but I was scared that this was just a fluke and I wouldn't be able to do it again tomorrow. This was what I was praying for. This was what I longed for. This was what I desperately needed, a small miracle that would get me through the day.

The next morning the first thing I did when I woke up was try and move that toe. It moved. I remember the look of excitement on my parents' face. For the last few weeks we had no positive news—everything was negative. With the slightest movement of this toe, I felt a switch in momentum; maybe we could really come back from this, maybe our family will make it through this. I felt it was time for a change in my own attitude too. So I stopped with the resistance and put on a smile (only if it was for brief periods of time). I continued to talk to God. I prayed the same prayer just about every day, "Dear Lord, thank you for the progress today, and if it's possible, could you send another small miracle my way tomorrow to help me make it through the day?" It was amazing to see what God was doing. One day a finger would move, the next day another toe would twitch. I was starting to get stronger, too. I was now able to push my wheelchair from my room all the way to therapy (granted, I was moving at tortoise speed, but it was still an accomplishment). My ab muscles were starting to reappear as well. I was now able to sit at the end of my bed by myself, and I didn't need to be strapped into my wheelchair anymore. After a few more weeks, I learned how to transfer from my hospital bed into my wheelchair—by myself. This was a huge accomplishment because I no longer needed to rely on people to get me in and out of bed. I was free. I could come and go as I please.

Chapter Eight

THE ESCAPE

I continued to gain strength in my upper body, but pushing around that stupid wheelchair was "a big pain in the you-know-what." Because I didn't have full use of my triceps and my right hand was still paralyzed, I wasn't able to keep my chair straight. I wasn't strong enough to push on a surface that was carpeted. My roommate Joe and I begged our therapist to give us a power chair for the weekend so we could get around easier. After weeks of nagging, they finally gave in and allowed us to use these high-powered motorized chairs for the weekend. It was awesome. I hadn't felt this free in a long time. I could go wherever I wanted and no one was going to stop me. The first thing Joe and I decided to do was to take these things outside. We had to be careful and sneak by the nurses because we were not allowed to be outside without supervision. We both crept by the nurses' station unnoticed. We made it to the elevators and searched for the ground floor button. This proved difficult because both our hands were paralyzed and we couldn't use our fingers to hit the button. I'm not sure how we got the elevator to start going down, but I have a feeling we "conned" some poor unsuspecting individual into pressing "G" for us. Next we had to make it past the front desk and security guards. This wasn't very hard because the lobby was a busy place and we were so low to the ground we were tough to spot. The doors were in sight. I hit the power button and pushed through the front door. We made it. We had escaped from 7A. The feeling of being outside after all that time was indescribable. The warm June air felt amazing as it touched my face. For the first time in a long time I felt alive. I felt human again.

Once we made it outside, we weren't quite sure what we were going to do. We looked at each other and said, "Let's go to the parking lot." This probably wasn't the best idea because neither one of us really knew how to drive these chairs, plus it would have been pretty easy for one of us to get smashed by some random car driving by. Oh, well, I was twenty-one and it sounded cool at the time. We made our way up the deck and cruised back and forth through the different sections. It felt so good. I couldn't stop smiling. I'm sure Joe felt the same way. As we made our way down the last area of the parking deck, we came across the exit tunnel that led onto the street. This was a pretty steep hill that was not the easiest to walk, let alone get a wheelchair down. We looked at each other, "First one to the road wins!" We took off. Two paralyzed rebels traveling at extreme high speed down a concrete hill with absolutely no cares whatsoever. We were searching for any opportunity to act like normal immature twentysomething-year-old kids. I can only imagine what the security guards were thinking as Joe and I flew past their station and onto the busy road in front of the hospital. We didn't care. This was our weekend and we were on a mission.

After we got ourselves regrouped from our daredevil ride, we contemplated on what we should do next. For some odd reason we came up with the idea to go downstairs and look for the morgue. I don't know why we decided to do this or what we hoped to accomplish by finding it, but it sounded like a good plan at the time. We had no idea where we were going but somehow found our way to the basement. For the life of me I can't remember if we actually found the morgue or not, but I can tell you we had a blast searching for it.

About the same time some of my friends came up to visit me from back home. It was so good to see these guys, I missed them so much. We were sitting up in our room and talking about things back home. At some point during their visit I remembered that there was a corner grocery store about a block away from the hospital. I really wanted a beer and convinced my friends that it would be a good idea to venture over there and grab a six-pack. So here we go again. We rolled outside and onto the streets of Cleveland in search of a cold drink. We found the store and one by one made our way through the narrow entrance. When it was my turn, my friend tried to push me through the door but I wouldn't fit, my chair being too wide. No big deal, I just hollered out my order, "Grab me a six of brew!" I'm sure the store clerk had never seen something like this before. We had to smuggle the beer back into our room so the nurses wouldn't catch us. I'm sure my doctors would not have been too thrilled with me washing down all those pills I was taking with a cold beer. I stashed it in my closet and waited until evening time. Finally later on that night, I cracked open my first beer. It was awesome—now I feel twenty-one again. After I finished the few bottles of beer for the night, I found out one of the reasons why doctors frown upon alcohol consumption by those paralyzed. Remember that catheter I was telling you about earlier? Well, the more I drank the more fluids my body produced. Eventually the fluid intake became too much for my bladder to handle. I'm pretty sure the nurses knew I was drinking but they were all really understanding about it.

I loved all of my nurses on the Spinal Cord Unit. They were so nice and really bonded with my family and me. I remember one of my nurses (whom I seemed to only have at night) was one of my favorites. One evening we got to talking and she told me she was a Wicca. I had no idea what that was, I just figured she was some type of witch or something. Then she proceeded to tell me that she could see people who have passed away. I started to get a bit anxious. I asked, "You mean you can see dead people just walking around the building?" She said, "Sure, I see them all the time! Don't worry most of them are nice." Wow! I acted tough, but inside I was as scared as an eight-year-old little girl. She continued to share stories like that with me from time to time—it was "unusual" but made for interesting conversation at 12:00 at night.

Another Sunday morning rolled around and Joe and I were back in our power chairs. We enjoyed our time and got to spend some time with patients whom we really didn't know that well. On Monday morning we woke up to our normal routine. We asked if our power chairs were still out in the hallway. Now, I don't know how much of our weekend adventure was actually known by the hospital staff, but all I know is we were never given those fun toys again. It was back to our old, boring manual chairs.

Aside from the occasional weekend slipup, therapy was going great and I was starting to develop my relationship with Jesus. One day the hospital chaplain came into my room and had a conversation with me. He was nice, not pushy at all. I also found out the hospital had a church service on Sunday mornings. I didn't particularly like to attend church services, but Joe and I decided to go check it out. I didn't have a life-changing "Pauline" (road to Damascus) type of transformation, but I do believe God was slowly starting to "chisel away" the hard parts of my heart.

Chapter Nine

PREPPING TO COME HOME

A s I was approaching two-and-a-half months in the hospital, my case manager wanted me to start thinking about my new life at home. Although I had made some miraculous strides in my recovery, it looked as if I was going to fall short of the goal I set to walk out of the hospital. As much as I didn't want to acknowledge it, I had to come to terms with the reality that I was going home in a wheelchair and was going to be stuck in it for some time. So now was the time I needed to decide what make, model, and color I wanted. This was one of the hardest realities I have ever had to face. After I decided on my chair, we had to have something called a "family meeting." This was a gathering of all my doctors, nurses, and therapists, and they consulted my family on what to expect when we leave the hospital and transition into the home. By the end of the meeting I was in tears. I couldn't believe the stuff they were talking about. All of these people were discussing the next eighty years of my life and I had absolutely no say in it whatsoever.

One of the ways they help you adjust to life in a wheelchair is an "outing." They get all the patients on the unit together and then vote on where they wanted to have a day trip. We had a few suggestions thrown out, but the consensus was we would take two tips—one to the zoo, and one to the Science Center. The trips were fun, but it was clear that our lives would be different forever. We all loaded onto the handicapped accessible vans and they strapped each one of us in. After we arrived, they unloaded us and we headed to the entrance. One of the hardest things to get used to being in a chair is the constant stares. Most of the time it is just kids being curious, but occasionally you get the adult who just can't take their eyes off the "quad in the wheelchair." I learned pretty quickly to develop a thick skin. Sometimes if I caught someone staring at me for an extended period of time, I would just stare right back at them until they became uncomfortable and turned away.

Another way they tried to get us used to being in social settings was to organize games for all the patients and their families. Normally I would have nothing to do with playing games like "bingo or charades," but all it takes is the right motivation and a young man will do just about anything. Towards the end of my stay at MetroHealth, they brought on a new intern who was studying to be a recreational therapist. She was very outgoing and really hot! One afternoon after Joe and I had finished eating, she came into our room and asked us if we wanted to participate in the daily activity. I politely declined, but she wasn't taking no for an answer. She dragged Joe and me down to join the rest of the patients and it turned out to be a lot of fun. As the weeks went on, she and I got pretty close. She would make sure I was at every event that she was coordinating and would come and hang out in my room when she had a break. Usually I was pretty good when it came to the ladies but since my accident, I didn't have much confidence and felt like "I lost my game." She was great, though: she never treated me like I was some charity case in a chair, she treated me like a normal guy (a guy who just so happened to be hitting on her). This was an important step in my life: I realized that "girls dig guys in wheelchairs"; maybe I didn't have to be alone; maybe I wasn't destined to live with my mommy for the rest of my life.

And we kept in contact after I left the hospital; in fact she was my first date (and kiss) since my accident!

As going home was getting closer and closer, I was attacking my last days of therapy with everything I had. I was starting to make great strides and regaining some muscle function that I had lost. I was now able to sit up by myself, I had some movement back in my legs, and I could stand with a lot of assistance. My next challenge was to try and take a few steps inside the parallel bars. As I continued to get stronger, my therapist warmed up to the idea of me giving the bars a shot. I was really excited because my college basketball coach had driven up to Cleveland to visit me. This gave me even more of a determination as I loved my coach and did not want to fail in front of him. My coach came into the therapy clinic and sat down near the middle of the bars. My therapist wheeled me over to the right side of the parallel bars and locked my chair into place. They lifted me out of the chair and I was grasping the bars as tightly as I could. I still remember what I was wearing—black athletic pants with a white shirt. My neck brace was covering the front of my shirt. I was scared; I braced myself as Deb told me to take a step forward. I tried to move my right leg but it wasn't really working. Deb grabbed it and moved it forward for me. Then it was time to move my left leg. I took a breath and pushed forward—it moved! I tried to move my right leg again, same result—Deb needed to help me. Now it was time for "lefty" again: I pushed forward and my left leg swung through. We continued this pattern all the way to the end of the bars. I couldn't believe it—I took a few steps! My exhausted body crashed back into my wheelchair. Immediately my coach came over and congratulated me. I wish I could remember what he said to me, but I am sure it was exactly what I needed to hear. It was a strange feeling to be standing up again. One of my therapists made the comment that "I didn't know you were so tall—I am used to seeing you sitting down."

Mark 2:1–12: "A few days later, when Jesus again entered Capernaum, the people heard that He had come home. So many gathered that there was no room left, not even outside the door, and He preached the word to them. Some men came, bringing to Him a paralytic, carried by four of them. Since they could not get him to Jesus because of the crowd, they made an opening in the roof above Jesus and, after digging through it, lowered the mat the paralyzed man was lying on. When Jesus saw their faith, He said to the paralytic, Son your sins are forgiven.

Now some teachers of the law were sitting there, thinking to themselves, why does this fellow talk like that? He's blaspheming! Who can forgive sins but God alone? Immediately Jesus knew in His spirit that this was what they were thinking in their hearts, and He said to them, Why are you thinking these things? Which is easier: to say to the paralytic, Your sins are forgiven, or to say, Get up, take your mat and walk? But that you may know that the Son of Man has authority on earth to forgive sins… He said to the paralytic, I tell you, get up, take your mat and go home. He got up took his mat and walked out in full view of them all. This amazed everyone and they praised God, saying we have never seen anything like this!"

When I read stories in the Bible like this about Jesus healing people from their paralysis, I wonder if they had a similar feeling. I wonder how long this guy was paralyzed? I wonder what was going through his head after Jesus healed him? I have a feeling he probably grabbed his mat and took off back home running, jumping, and praising God for this amazing miracle. I was by no means completely healed like the man in the Bible, but I did experience a miraculous change.

I still don't fully understand why I was lucky enough to be able to get up out of my chair while so many people can't. I know for a fact there are WAY better people than me who are confined to their wheelchairs for the rest of their lives. These people are paralyzed because of illness, accident, or even senseless violence—I was paralyzed because I was out drinking with my friends. It doesn't make sense and it doesn't seem fair. I will carry a sense of guilt and sadness with me for the rest of my life. Now that God had given me such an amazing gift, what was I going to do with it?

Chapter Ten

COMING HOME WITH FOUR WHEELS

The day I left the hospital to come was bittersweet. I was really excited to come home and see all my friends and family, but I was going to miss all my new friends I made in Cleveland. I was also nervous about all this medical stuff that my family and I would now be responsible for. What if something went wrong? My house was a long way from Cleveland, and I was pretty sure my primary physician would not be up to date on how to take care of a C5 quadriplegic. As we were packing up my room, I got a chance to sit back and reflect on the last three months of my life. It was surreal. So many people had been there for me. So many people lent me a hand in my darkest hour. We started to put what seemed to be hundreds of cards that people had sent me into a box (I still have those today and treasure them dearly). After loading the last of my belongings into our vehicle, there was only one thing left to do: say goodbye. Leaving these awesome people was extremely difficult. I had grown to love and cherish many of those people at Metro (except the nurse who wrote me up for being "unruly"—kidding, I love you too!) I gave them all hugs and assured them I would stay in touch. I exchanged numbers with a few of them (especially the Wicca—she was cool!) in hopes of grabbing a drink sometime. I rolled down the hall of floor 7A for the last time as a patient. As soon as I went out the door my family and I were on our own, left to ourselves to embark on a journey of a lifetime!

Prior to me leaving the hospital, my family had to do a lot of work to make our family home accessible for a quadriplegic. Many modifications needed to take place in order for me to be able to just to get in and out of our home safely. One of the major renovations that needed to be done to the house was the addition of a wheelchair ramp. This proved to be a difficult task, as our home was a split-level. I could easily get into the basement area, but if I wanted to spend any time upstairs we needed a ramp. Luckily for me, my brother and dad were both handy when it came to building things. The ramp was a massive undertaking. It needed to be quite long in order for it to wrap all the way around the house and reach our entrance on the back porch. My family did a great job on it and it worked well. Plus, all the neighborhood kids loved it because they could ride their bikes up and down it and pretend they were professional dirt bike riders.

We also had to rip up all the carpet off the floor so I could push my chair around. I had a hard enough time pushing on a hard level surface, there was no way my "puny little quad arms" could push through thick carpeting. We also had to widen some of the doors in the house because my wheelchair had some special modifications to it that made it impossible to get through doorways. One of these doorways was to the bathroom. For three months I had to use the restroom with the door open. Praise Jesus I had understanding women living in my house.

Trying to adjust to my new life in a wheelchair.

Another facet of moving back home involved dealing with was the massive amount of medical equipment that continued to pile up around the house. Besides my chair, it seemed like almost every room I spent any considerable amount of time in needed to have some type of medical device in it. I loved being home, but looking around at all that medical junk made me feel like I was right back at the hospital.

Along with all the clutter accumulating in our house, I had to get used to relying on my family to be my primary caretakers from now on. This was a really big adjustment for me. It was bad enough that I still had to use catheters and suppositories, but now my parents were the ones who would be helping me use them. I remember sitting in the middle of my bedroom one evening after my dad had helped me with what I still call "my bathroom stuff"—I was blown away at how big of a turn my life had taken over the last few months. I felt like I lost all my self-respect. I was twenty-one years old sitting on a bathroom chair in my bedroom waiting for my mom to check my bowel movement to make sure everything looked "normal."

Normal! Nothing about this new life remotely resembled anything normal. I know this sounds really selfish and ungrateful (because at that moment my roommate Joe was stuck in some nursing home with people four times his age), but I couldn't live the rest of my life like this, could I?

One of the ways I could escape from everything going on with my health was a night out with my friends. I had some great friends who stuck through everything with me and were always there for me when I needed a night out on the town. Going out on a Friday night used to be so easy—I could just throw on some clothes, grab a few drinks, and hop into the car and away I went! Not so easy anymore. Getting ready was a huge chore. Just to get myself ready to go was a process. I needed my mom to help me get ready, my dad to get me out the door, and my friends to load me into their car. Although it was a hassle, once I was out of the house it felt like old times. We would laugh and made fun of each other (because that's what you do when you're twenty-one), and plan out our night ahead. There were some perks of going to bars in a wheelchair. I almost always got to go to the front of the line; I guess people felt bad that the guy in the chair had to stand out in the snow. I would also get a lot of free drinks. Total strangers would come up to me with tears in their eyes and want to do a shot with me. That was always kind of strange to me but hey, I was not going to pass up a free drink. And the best part of being in a chair at a bar was the women. I was desperate for some female attention and I was not too proud or ashamed to play the sympathy card. It was a great way to strike up conversation with girls who would otherwise probably not have anything to do with me. This is the only time I felt alive—the more I drank, the more I didn't care that I was paralyzed.

I remember one of these particular evenings very well.

This was the night that God "smacked me in the face" and helped me realize I had some serious issues with alcohol. This night started out just like all the other ones. I was hanging out at a local bar with all my best friends. The night was going great and we were all having lots of fun. There was a set of speakers set up at the front of this establishment and we were playing all of our favorite jams. At some point we decided it would be a good idea to start doing shots. This was one of the first times since I got out of the hospital that I drank this heavily. I was consuming anything that was placed in front of me. Towards the end of the evening I realized that I was drunk, and I mean really drunk. Normally I wouldn't care: I would just have my friends drop me off at my apartment and that would be the end of it. Things were different now; I lived with my parents and getting past them and up into my bed was going to be difficult. We finally left the bar and headed for home. Because of the level of my intoxication, my brother picked me up and headed into our home. I pleaded with him to just put me on the couch downstairs and I assured him I would be okay. He couldn't do it; he wanted to make sure I was okay, so he headed quietly up the stairs with me in his arms. As we were about to hit the second floor, the lights turned on and there she was—it was my mother and she was not happy. She started yelling at my brother and friends and screamed at them, "How could you let him get like this?" Little did my mom know that I was the idiot throwing down massive amounts of hard liquor all night. My dad then grabbed me and picked me up out of my brother's arms and put me into my bed. I was furious at my parents for making such a big deal about this. I yelled at them and told them, "I was moving out!" I couldn't believe I was treating my family this way. These are the people who were there for me at my darkest hour. The people who took care of me and were there whenever I needed them. They didn't deserve this!

I continued to live this way for almost a year. I had a set schedule of going out drinking every night of the week. Sunday night was bowling night. We would grab a couple pitchers of beer and chuck some bowling balls down the lane. Monday night was wrestling night. We would gather at someone's house or a restaurant and watch *The match*. Tuesday night was my favorite night because we went to the local bar, the Canal Boat Lounge. This place was awesome, 65 cent draft beers and cheap shots. Wednesday night was our country night out at the Saloon (remember the establishment I celebrated my twenty-first birthday at?). Thursday night we went to a night club at Kent State University. This place was fun because my sister lived in one of the sorority houses and would introduce me to all her good-looking friends. Friday and Saturday nights were open to whatever. Most of the time we would meet at a friend's house and play pool for a while, before heading out to a bar of some kind. Now don't get me wrong: my friends and I had a great time and made some amazing memories, *but I was still searching for something more.* I still felt empty and hollow inside. It didn't matter how many drinks I had or how many women I hooked up with, I had a desire for something real, something pure, something that couldn't be satisfied by my lustful desires.

Psalm 51:10–13: "Create in me a pure heart, O God, and renew a steadfast spirit within me. Do not cast me from your presence or take your Holy Spirit from me. Restore to me the joy of your salvation and grant me a willing spirit, to sustain me."

As much as I desired a pure heart, I could not break the hold that sin had on my life. I seemed to be spiraling out of control with no way to slow down. To make matters worse, I was not only abusing alcohol, I also had a massive supply of prescription drugs at my disposal. Anything I needed I would just ask my doctor for and he would write me a prescription. I learned pretty quickly that a cocktail of prescription drugs and alcohol can be a dangerous combination. One summer weekend I decided I to visit one of my college friends back at Edison. It was great to be back at campus and I enjoyed running into some of my old friends. One night as we were sitting around the table, I brought out a bag of about thirty or so muscle relaxants. For some reason we thought it would be a good idea to cut the pills up (similar to cocaine) and sniff them through our noses. We discovered this was a quick way to achieve a new kind of buzz without having to consume as much alcohol. After a few minutes passed, one of the men at the table asked me if I would be willing to trade my bag of muscle relaxants for a bag of marijuana. To me it was a no-brainer. I would have more pills in a matter of days so I might as well trade them so I could enjoy some delicious cannabis. It seemed so innocent at the time; no one would get hurt, we were just having a good time. Thinking back in my life, this is one of those decisions that still haunt me. I have no idea what that man did with those pills. I don't know what he was passing them off as. For all I know someone could have been seriously hurt or even killed because of my irresponsibility. I still live with the guilt from that decision. I have since repented to Jesus for my actions, but I couldn't live with myself if someone was hurt because of my carelessness.

This brings me to my next story and the start of God's transformation in my life.

I was fascinated by this new life I was living. Prescription drugs and alcohol seemed so cool to me. I loved the feeling I would get when I brought out that little bag of pills and proceeded to show them how to sniff the medication to achieve the ultimate buzz. I didn't know it at the time, but I was nothing more than a drug dealer. I exchanged my medicines for some type of financial or other gain. One night as we were mixing pills, marijuana, and alcohol, one of my friends became noticeably intoxicated. As the night progressed, he could barely walk and was having trouble lying flat. I knew it was because of my pills. After a year of use, I had built up a resistance to the medication so I was able to handle the large doses—my friend was not. We helped this young man to bed and continued to party. Later on in the evening my friend called out to me and asked me to come into his room. I found him lying on his floor in terrible shape. He was pleading with me to take him to the emergency room. I knew what would happen if we went to the hospital: the police would ask him where he got the pills from and I knew I would get busted. I remember taking one last look at my friend in need and shutting the door on him. I don't know if I ever checked on him the rest of the night. He could have died that night and it would have been all my fault. I didn't care, all I was concerned with was myself. What would make me happy in the moment. The next morning when I woke up and realized what I had done I was overcome with guilt and remorse. I couldn't believe that I was capable of doing that to anyone, let alone one of my best friends. That was it, I was done; I couldn't take this worthless life anymore. If I continued on this path, I was going to hurt or even kill someone. I needed help and I needed it now!

So one evening when I was home by myself, I went to the only person I thought was capable of helping me in my time of crisis— Jesus Christ. I hit my knees and hit them hard. I pleaded with God and told Him I needed help. I said I couldn't do this life alone and needed someone to come alongside me to help me change. It was a simple but powerful prayer. I had drawn a line in the sand—I had only ever prayed like this one time before and when I did it, not long after I got into my accident.

As all of this craziness was going on, I began to make some amazing progress in therapy. I was now able to stand on my own and take a few steps with a walker. I was getting stronger by the day and starting to spend less and less time in my wheelchair. A few months later I was able to walk without the assistance of any device. I couldn't believe it—I was walking! I was blown away by this whole experience; why was I in the 10 percent who are able to get up out of their chairs? Why was God rewarding me when it seemed like I was as far away from Him as humanly possible? There had to be a reason and I needed to find out the answer.

After I was able to walk with more confidence and regained the ability to take care of all my medical needs independently, I decided it was time for a vacation. I needed to get away for a while and decide what I was going to do with the rest of my life. I booked a hotel at one of my favorite places in the world, Myrtle Beach. I decided to take this vacation alone. I wanted to prove to myself that I could function by myself and didn't need anyone to help me. As I packed up my car, I had in my mind that I was going to South Carolina to have a great time and look for a permanent place to live. I wanted to find a job and a place to work.

After I made it down safely to South Carolina, I checked myself into my room, filled my fridge up with beer, and headed to the beach. I found a nice place to put my towel down and sunk into the hot sand. I grabbed my headphones and popped in my Myrtle Beach CD for the week, 50 Cent's "Get Rich or Die Trying." As I lost myself in the music, I closed my eyes and enjoyed the freedom. This felt like a million years away from my cold hospital room in Cleveland, Ohio. It was a beautiful June day and the temperature continued to rise. I felt my skin start to darken by the minute. This was about as perfect as it could get. But it was about to get better.

I happen to open my eyes for a second and saw this beautiful, dark-haired girl headed my way. She was wearing a yellow and red bikini (it's funny what your mind can remember). She spoke to me but I really had no idea what she was saying. Then I noticed she had a bottle of sunscreen in her hand. She spoke again, "Hi, my mom sent me over here because she thought you were getting a little red—do you want some sunscreen?" I searched for a cool answer but probably said something stupid. She introduced herself and told me her name was Rachel and she lived in Maryland. She and her mom were on a mother-daughter trip that they take each year. She sat down on my towel and we talked for a while; for the next three days we were inseparable.

I feel like God put Rachel in my life for a purpose. I learned quite a bit from our three days together. For the last few years I didn't respect women very much. I went to bars, drank a whole bunch, and started telling them a bunch of lies that I felt would give me the best chance to take them home. Rachel was different: she demanded respect! We spent time together and went on dates (real dates, not some dirty nightclub). I hung out in her hotel room and her mom was right there beside us eating lunch or telling me about their life back home. One evening Rachel and I went to The Landing, where we sat on the bench and talked for hours. She didn't care that I was limping around and had only one arm that worked, she seemed to genuinely like me and wanted to spend time together. We got really close over the next few days. When it was time for Rachel to leave I was sad, but I was extremely grateful that God had put someone in my life like her to teach me how to respect and care for a women. God knew what He was doing—He was working on my heart, preparing me for the woman who was about to walk into my life and change everything forever.

When I got back from South Carolina I started to get my life back together. I got my own apartment, enrolled in college, and I even returned to the basketball court as a freshman coach. For the first time in a long time I was enjoying life. At this time, I was doing outpatient physical therapy to strengthen the muscles that returned from my accident. One of my therapists at the clinic, Rose, became like a second mom to me. Not only was she an amazing therapist, she helped heal my soul as well. Rose talked to me about Jesus and how He could transform your life if you let Him. I listened intently as she spoke with such confidence through our 45-minute sessions. She had a light about her, a happiness that was able to drown out all the darkness in this sinful world. I wanted what she had; I wanted that relationship Rose had with God. I thought to myself, *After everything you have done in your life, why would God ever want anything to do with you?*

Besides being a therapist, Rose was also employed by a local college as a physical therapy assistant instructor. One day she asked me if I would be willing to come into her class and talk about my experience with my injury. I agreed to do it, but I was really scared. I didn't like to talk in front of large groups of people, but for Rose I would do it. The day of my talk came and I hobbled to the front of the class. I started talking about the importance of physical therapy assistants and how they were instrumental in my recovery. As I was talking, I couldn't help but notice this gorgeous blonde sitting in the front row. I finished my talk and asked Rose who that girl in the front right corner chair was. She then proceeded to tell me that her name was Suzie, but she had a boyfriend. Although I was bummed to hear that news, this would not be the last time Suzie and I crossed paths.

Chapter Eleven

THE RIVERTREE
EXPERIENCE

As some positive things were starting to evolve in my life, I could no longer deny that God was doing something in my life—but what? At the urging of some important people in my life, I decided it was time to try out a church. It had been a long time since I stepped foot inside of a church, but I decided to give it a try. The first few churches I tried out were cool. The people were friendly and the buildings were really big. I liked that these churches had multiple services because I was usually out late the night before so I enjoyed the late Sunday start time. To be honest, the first few times I went I was probably hungover, so I really wasn't into hearing some guy talk for 35 minutes. I bounced around from church to church hoping to find one that would appeal to me and was willing to accept the baggage I was carrying around.

Then one Sunday morning I found myself at Rivertree Christian Church. As soon as I walked into the building, I could feel something was different about this place. The service started with the worship music. It wasn't the old hymns and organ I was used to growing up. These guys were rocking out with guitars and a drum set. I felt the energy from the congregation. They had their hands up high as if they were reaching up to heaven. They knew every word to the songs and were singing them as if Jesus himself were standing next to them. Next, the pastor took the stage and welcomed everyone, "Good morning and welcome to Rivertree—I don't care where you're from or what you've done in your past, you are welcome here. Rivertree is a church that anyone can come to!" Did he say *anyone*? Certainly not me. If this pastor knew the horrible things I've done in my past, he would throw my paralyzed self out as quickly as I came in. He kept speaking. I hung on his every word. It sounded as if he were speaking directly to me. After he finished the sermon, he prayed and that was it. I was blown away! I wanted to hear more.

I continued to come back week after week. It was getting easier with each service I attended. I started to get to know a few people. They would ask me how I was doing. They would go out of their way to make me feel comfortable. No one was judging me. No one cared what I did in my past. The focus wasn't on me, it was on Jesus! Although I knew nothing about the Bible, I started to hear names of individuals and stories that I recognized. I heard stories about these people in the Bible who did horrible things in their past but went on to know Jesus and He used them to do great things. I heard about this guy named Moses who killed someone and then went on to deliver his people out of Egypt. Then there was this king named David who fell in love with a married woman and had her husband killed in battle. David went on to become a great king and devoted himself to serving God. Then there was my favorite. I heard about this man named Saul who went around persecuting the early Christians and putting them in jail. Then one day he had this amazing transformation and turned his life around. He went on to be a great apostle and wrote half of the New Testament. I thought to myself, *Hey, if Jesus could use these guys who have done terrible things in their past to further His Kingdom, maybe He could use me too!* I started to pray all the time. I asked for forgiveness for all the sins I committed in the past. I asked for forgiveness for all the people I've hurt. I was ready to surrender my life to Christ, but could I really do it?

It was during this time in my life that a familiar face walked back into my life. Suzie, the really hot blonde who I saw in therapy class had broken up with her boyfriend and for some reason wanted to meet me. Through the help of a friend, we went out on a group date. These types of dates are typically weird and awkward because there are a lot of people and it's hard to get the opportunity to spend any one-on-one time together. The date was awesome and it was evident that Suzie and I really liked each other from the start. The next day I called her and asked her to come over. To my surprise she agreed and we hung out all day. During the next couple weeks our relationship grew stronger and stronger. We were together all the time. We talked about everything. She was so cool with all my health issues and limitations that come along with being a quadriplegic. I knew that I loved this girl and wanted to spend the rest of my life with her, but I figured I better ask her to be my girlfriend first After less than a month of dating, we were already talking about getting married. I couldn't believe this was happening—I never thought I would be getting this serious with a girl I've only known for a month. I didn't care, I was in love and I was going to do whatever it took to put a ring on her finger.

During the next couple months a lot of changes took place inside of me. I stopped doing most of the bad stuff that kept getting me into trouble in my life. And the best part was Suzie never asked me to. I just wanted to change. I felt like in order for me to be around this amazing girl, I needed to change my life. Suzie grew up in the church so she knew all about God and how Christ followers were supposed to live. She was involved with her church youth group and sang in the worship band. The first time I heard her sing, I almost burst into tears. She was phenomenal. I remember telling her she needed to try out for *reality television*. I also spent a lot of time with her parents. I would stop over at her house after she got home from work and spend all evening with her family. I don't know if they knew what to make of me or not. I was four years older than Suzie, I had no real job, I was living off the government, and to top it off, I was paralyzed.

The next four months Suzie and I continued to get closer. We talked about our future together. I told her within the next month I was going to propose to her. My mom and dad knew how serious our relationship was getting. They were so happy for me. One Sunday morning in December, I asked my parents to go engagement ring-shopping because I had no idea what I was doing. My mom was great. She walked me through the entire ring-buying process. All I knew was I wanted to get a ring with her birthstone (sapphire) in it. Finally we found it! It was perfect, and I knew Suzie would love it. Now the only thing left to do was propose.

I searched for the right time to do something romantic that Suzie would really be impressed with. Suzie knew the ring was coming but was getting anxious because I was slow to pull the trigger (but come on, give some grace—I'm a guy!) I don't know how I eventually came up with this master plan, but I was rather impressed by my creativity. One evening I picked Suzie up after work; she was in a bad mood and I wondered if it was the right time to ask her or not. We got into my car and I told her we were meeting my friends from college that night for dinner. As we were driving to the restaurant, I acted like I forgot something at my apartment and told her I needed to stop by. Earlier that day I had placed about a million candles all around my apartment. I also went and bought a dozen roses that I placed on my bed and had a radio with our favorite song all queued up and ready to play. So I ran into my apartment, lit the candles, and turned on our song (Tim McGraw's "Best Friend"). After everything was set up, I ran back outside and told her I needed help with something inside. She looked annoyed—she had no idea what I had in store for her inside.

As she walked into my beautiful candlelit apartment she started to smile; she knew what was going on. I led her through the apartment and into my bedroom. I had her sit on the bed as I knelt on the floor.

I started to read her a poem that I had written her in anticipation for this moment. I was really nervous but got through it. At the end of the poem I reached into my nightstand and pulled out the ring. I was shaking as I looked up at her and somehow uttered the words **"Um, will you marry me?"** She gave me an emphatic "Yes!" I placed the ring on her finger and wondered how in the world I got this amazing woman to agree to marry me (it could only be God!).

We set a date to get married a year from our engagement. This gave our families some time to get over the "shock value" of our announcement. Over that year I really made some progress in my walk with God. I continued going to church every week and was even starting to read the Bible. I also started to look for ways to get involved with our church. I helped out with a car show and signed up to deliver Thanksgiving meals to people in need. I started to attend a monthly men's group on the first Saturday of every month. I was loving this! Something unexplainable was happening inside of me: I was starting to let go of some of that guilt that I had been carrying around for years. I was slowly walking away from some of the bad habits that got me into trouble in the past. I wasn't staying out late on Saturday nights as much anymore because I made it a priority to be at church the next morning. I felt different inside—like that dark empty place that had taken control of my body was starting to dissipate.

As much as I was progressing spiritually in my life, I still carried around a lot of guilt and pride from the life I used to live. No matter what I tried, it would not go away completely. This became a big problem for me because I never felt good enough to truly call myself a Christ Follower. I think this is the first time I realized how powerful the devil really is. I felt like Satan was doing everything he could to keep me away from Jesus and pull me back into the darkness of my old life. Then one day I heard my pastor talking about baptism. He said it was a way to publicly declare your love for Jesus and announce to the world that you are one of His followers. I was intrigued by the idea of it, but I thought I couldn't do it because I was already baptized as a baby. The pastor then went on to tell us that we should be thankful we had parents who loved us enough to baptize us as children, but now that we are adults we have the opportunity to make the decision for ourselves. I was sold! *I wanted to do this. I needed to do this.*

It reminded me of one of my favorite stories in the Bible:

Acts 8:26–38: "Now an angel of the Lord said to Philip, 'Go south to the road—the desert road—that goes down from Jerusalem to Gaza.' So he started out, an on his way he met an Ethiopian Eunuch, an important official in charge of all the treasury of Candace, queen of the Ethiopians. This man had gone to Jerusalem to worship, and on his way home was sitting in his chariot reading the book of Isaiah the prophet. The sprit told Philip, 'Go to that chariot and stay near it.' Then Philip ran to the chariot and heard the man reading Isaiah the prophet. 'Do you understand what you are reading?' Philip asked. 'How can I,' he said, 'unless someone explains it to me?' So he invited Philip to come up and sit with him.

The Eunuch was reading this passage of scripture:

'He was led like a sheep to the slaughter,

And as a lamb before the shearer is silent,

So he did not open his mouth.

In his humiliation he was deprived of justice.

Who can speak of his descendants?

For his life was taken from the earth.'

The Eunuch asked Philip, 'Tell me, please, who is the prophet talking about, himself or someone else?' Then Philip began with that very passage of Scripture and told him the good news about Jesus. As they traveled along the road, they came to some water and the eunuch said, 'Look here is some water. Why shouldn't I be baptized?' And he gave orders to stop the chariot. Then both Philip and the eunuch went down into the water and Philip baptized him."

I felt like that eunuch—I thought to myself, *Why shouldn't I be baptized?*

The day of the baptism came and I was nervous. I walked into the back of the church and took my place at the end of the long line of people who were committed to giving their lives to Christ. As I was walking, I recognized one of the men in line. "Wow, I didn't expect to see you here," I uttered. The last time I saw this guy I was consuming mass amounts of alcohol, smoking weed, and popping mushrooms—now we were both in line ready to get baptized (I love how God works!). I stood in line watching the crowd get smaller and smaller. It was almost my turn. I couldn't believe I was actually doing this. Right before it was my turn, Satan tried one more time to get me to bail. I remember thinking to myself, *I'm paralyzed. I don't even think I can get into the pool and even if I do manage to get in, how is this guy going to keep me from drowning?* I thought about calling the whole thing off. Then I spotted my fiancée; she came back to check on me and to see if I needed any help. That was all the assurance I needed. I was up next; I limped into the baptismal pool and whispered to the pastor, "Um, my legs don't really work—will you be able to hold me up?" He smiled at me and told me, "I got you!" He asked me a few questions about following Jesus and then he dunked me and gave me a huge hug. I looked out into the audience and saw the one person I invited standing there clapping for me. This was it, the start of a new life. I no longer had to do it alone—I had a helper—an advocate—I had the Holy Spirit!

Matthew 3:13–17: "Then Jesus came to Galilee to the Jordan to be baptized by John. But John tried to deter Him, saying, 'I need to be baptized by you, and do you come to me?' Jesus relied, 'Let it be so now; it is proper for us to do this to fulfill all righteousness.' Then John consented. As soon as Jesus was baptized, He went up out of the water. At that moment heaven was opened, and He saw the Spirit of God descending like a dove and lighting on Him. And a voice from heaven said, 'This is my son, whom I love; with Him I am well pleased.'"

I wish I could say all this cool stuff happened after my baptism, but it didn't. I wasn't able to hear the audible voice of God, but something miraculous did take place and I was now a changed man. I had given my life to Jesus, repented for all my sins, and had just gotten baptized. It was hard for me to believe that Jesus was just going to forgive me for all that junk I did in my past. But that's what He does. He delights when one of His children who has gone astray finds their way back home.

Matthew 18:12–13: "What do you think? If a man owns a hundred sheep, and one of them wanders away, will he not leave the ninety-nine on the hill and go to look for the one that wandered off? And if he finds it, I tell you the truth, he is happier about that one sheep than the ninety-nine that did not wander off."

After my baptism I started to examine my life. I wanted to address the areas in my life that were causing me to sin and keeping me from being the man that God created me to be. The first area of concern for me was my selfishness. Although I had made great strides in my walk with Christ, I was still a very prideful person. I craved attention from others and liked to hear people say nice things about me. This was becoming an issue for me because I found myself doing certain things just to get recognition and feel good about ME. Even as I was volunteering or giving to a needy cause, I still wanted people to notice what I was doing and give me some sort of praise for doing it. This destructive trait seemed to be ingrained in my personality at an early age. I can go all the way back to my basketball days and notice those same tendencies. It didn't matter if the team won or lost, all that mattered was how many points I scored and how big of a write-up I got in the newspaper. I wanted to do good things, but I was looking for a reward!

Matthew 6:1: "Be careful not to do your 'act of righteousness' before men, to be seen by them. If you do, you will have no reward from your Father in heaven."

Jesus goes on to call these people "hypocrites," and I was a prime example of one. You know one of those people who call themselves a "Christ Follower" but really do nothing but fuel that hypocritical stereotype Christ Followers have received over the last 2000 years. One day at church I heard about an organization called Compassion International. These people at Compassion seemed to really heave a heart and a passion for children living on the margins of society. I heard them talk about how impoverished these children were and the terrible conditions they were living in. I immediately became cynical. I've seen this before, some multimillion-dollar organization shows a picture of a few hungry kids and tugs on our heartstrings and then all of a sudden everyone's wallets magically open and mindlessly give money to the greedy CEOs. Normally about this time I would tune out, but for some reason I kept listening. I heard the speaker talk about these children not having a school to attend. I heard that these children didn't have any access to everyday basic medical necessities. Then I heard the statistic that wrecked my heart: most of these children will never have the opportunity to hear about Jesus. That was all I needed to hear. I couldn't believe these innocent little children living in extreme poverty may grow up and never experience the absolute joy of having a personal relationship with Jesus Christ. I was devastated. I was emotional. I was angry. Then they went on to show a video of what Compassion was doing in these Third World nations to try and make a change. I saw these little children wearing dirty clothes (that were three times too big for them) sitting in school houses smiling as they were being educated and getting the opportunity to hear about Jesus for the first time.

After the service, our pastor issued a challenge for every one of us to consider sponsoring one of these precious hurting children. I was ready. As soon as the service was over, I hobbled out of the auditorium and made my way over to the tables that Compassion had set up. Hundreds of child packets were spread across these tables; I wanted to sponsor them all—how would I ever choose one? I scanned up and down those tables multiple times. Then out of the corner of my eye I spotted her. She was a tiny little four-year-old girl from Chillca, Peru, wearing a brightly colored outfit with a pair of dirty old shoes. In her picture she tried her best to smile, but I could see the pain in her eyes right down into her soul. She was sad and needed help. There was no thought process, no consideration of the financial commitment, no worry about someone stealing my credit card information. I knew God placed this precious child in my life for a reason. Rosa (that was her name) was probably the first selfless decision I ever made. And that decision changed my life forever!

Chapter Twelve

OH, NO,
I'M GETTING MARRIED!

T he next year of my life went by fast. Suzie and I were busy getting ready for the wedding and finding a place to live. I also got a job working for a small computer repair business. It was an exciting and hectic time. A month before the wedding, my mom started to get sick. She spent a lot of time in and out of the hospital. We weren't sure what was wrong with her because her only symptom was a bad cough. As January 7th was fast approaching, Mom's health was going downhill quickly. She became so ill that she and my dad had to miss the night of the rehearsal dinner. It was hard not to have the two most important people in my lives at the dinner, but I understood why they couldn't make it.

Finally, the day of the wedding had arrived. I was excited and ready for Suzie to be my wife. I got to the church early along with all of my groomsmen. I remember trying to dress myself in this small little room that the church referred to as the "cry room." I tried my best to put on my tux but my paralyzed hand could not manipulate the buttons. As I slipped my dark black dress shoes over the brace I had to wear to help me walk, the reality of what was about to happen started to sink in. Could I actually be a good husband? Could I provide for my wife the way she deserved? Was I really as "changed of a man?" Well, I was about to find out.

My best friend and the most beautiful woman in the world—
I definitely married up!

As I stood at the front of the church waiting for Suzie, I glanced around to see all the people who had come out to celebrate this special day with us. It was overwhelming to see all these individuals who had stuck with me through everything I'd been through over the years. The music started. I felt a big lump in my throat and I made myself take a breath. Then, there she was, standing at the entrance ready to make the long walk down the aisle. She looked absolutely gorgeous, just like a princess! I couldn't believe this was happening. It wasn't that long ago that I was lying on my back paralyzed from the neck down not knowing if I were going to live or die.

I watched as it was time for the mothers to light the "unity candle." My mother had been sick for the last month and no one could figure out what was wrong. She could hardly walk. She grasped tightly to my mother-in-law's arm determined to make it without collapsing. I was so proud of her; this was as much her day as it was mine. The priest continued with the service. It came to the part where we were to exchange vows. We decided that we would write our own vows. It was a beautiful moment. I was in tears as soon as the priest began to read Suzie's heartfelt words. I peeked at the crowd and saw them crying, too. After we finished I kissed my new wife and walked up the aisle. We decided we wanted our exit to be candlelit. All our closest family and friends raised their lights as we walked by them for the first time as husband and wife. It was the perfect wedding and the perfect day.

As we reached the reception hall, I was ready to party. This was a celebration and I intended to make sure everyone had a great time. We danced, laughed, ate, and enjoyed a few cocktails (please don't try and debate responsible drinking and Christianity—friends, it's just not that clear). After we ate, it was approaching time for the mother-son dance. I talked to Dad a few minutes before and we both agreed Mom was too sick and weak to try and make it through the dance. I went over and gently broke the news to my mom. She was not having any of that and told me she WAS doing the dance and that was final. As the music began to play ("I Hope You Dance"), I had to hold this frail fragile woman tightly so she wouldn't collapse on the floor. She made it all the way through the dance with a big smile on her face. This is one of my fondest memories and I will cherish it forever.

As the night went on, the mood changed from one of pure joy to one of sadness and uncertainty. As I exited the bathroom, I noticed some of the ladies gathered in the lobby. A few of them were crying and some were embracing each other with hugs. I wasn't quite sure what to make of the scene and just assumed that everything was all right. By the end of the night everyone was ready to go to the hotel. We got into the limo and made the 20-minute journey to Akron. We had a Friday evening wedding (to keep costs down), so our flight to our honeymoon didn't leave until Sunday. This gave us a day to recuperate from the last few crazy weeks. At some point on Saturday, my mother was admitted into the hospital. Suzie and I asked her father if he would stop by the hospital on the way to the airport so I could check on mom. As I walked into the hospital room, my mother greeted me with a big smile. I asked her how she was doing and of course she said she was fine. She told us she had to have a hysterectomy and that once the operation was complete, she would be better. I had no clue what a hysterectomy was but I could tell she was downplaying the severity of it. She assured me she would be fine and urged us to get going to catch our plane.

Suzie and I decided to go to the island of Saint Lucia for our honeymoon. My parents went there a few years prior and had a great time. We stayed at a beautiful Caribbean Resort. The island was beautiful. I had never seen flowers that bright before. We met an awesome couple down there who were on their honeymoon, too. We spent much of the week together exploring the island and hanging out by the pool. It was exactly what we needed. Although I was having a dream vacation, I couldn't help but wonder how my mother was doing. It was difficult to call home because I didn't have a cell phone and it was crazy expensive to use the hotel phone. So I did what I knew my mom would want me to do—have fun! I didn't want to leave this island paradise or our new best friends, but I was anxious to get back and see my mom up out of that hospital bed.

When we arrived back home at the airport it was late. We had arranged for my dad to pick us and take us back to his house (even though Suzie and I were married, we still were living with my parents while our house was being built). It was strange to see my sister with my dad. It was a quite ride home, and something didn't feel right. I had a feeling something was going on with Mom but I was scared to ask. Finally I broke the awkward silence and asked the question—"So, how is Mom?" There was a pause for a moment, and then I heard the words I feared the most: "Brian, your mom has *cancer!*"

Now, I have a feeling this was not a new development. My mom knew if I found out she had cancer before my honeymoon I never would have gone. I'm sure she didn't want me to worry about her and she was trying to protect me. That's what I love about mothers: even in their darkest hour, even when they are facing their toughest challenge, they are always trying to protect their children. It took me awhile to grasp the severity of the situation. The next day I rushed into the hospital room to see my mom and tell her all about my trip. I didn't get it. I looked at this woman and she did not appear to be sick at all. The next day the doctor called us all into a meeting room to discuss my mother's health. She told us that Mom had a rare and fast-moving type of cancer. She said that chemo and transplants were not an option. The cancer was too strong to fight and within a few weeks she would die.

This news devastated our family. They moved her from her hospital room to a nearby hospice facility. I remember walking out behind my mother to the ambulance and, looking back, I saw a nurse *weeping* and needing to be comforted by another employee. This whole thing did not make any sense. My mom was way too young to die. She had so much left to give to this world. I needed my mom. I was only twenty-five years old—how was I supposed to continue on?

I was never mad at God for the cancer. I could tell I was changing, I could tell I was a new person. The old Brian would not have taken this news so well. The old Brian would have punched a doctor or gotten so hammered that I didn't care about anything. I felt calmness about the whole thing. Like God had everything in control and all I had to do was trust Him. Although I was young in my walk with Christ, God used this opportunity to teach me about His sovereignty.

Revelation 7:17: "For the lamb at the center of the throne will be their shepherd; He will lead them to springs of living water. And God will wipe away every tear from their eye."

Over the next two weeks I slowly watched the evil that is cancer ravish my poor mother's body. She no longer looked like Mom. Her face was sunken in so far that I could see her cheekbones. Her skin and eyes had both turned yellow from the damage to her kidneys. She hurt all over and was suffering greatly. I wanted so badly to cuddle up next to her in that small hospice bed. The nurse told us to keep the touching to a minimum because even the smallest touch would cause her distress. It was a helpless feeling. She did her best to hang on, but it was almost time for her to go back home and be with Jesus.

After two weeks in hospice my family was told to rush into my mother's room because she only had a few minutes left. We all gathered around her and listened to her breathing become more and more labored. I glanced around the room and saw all the people who my mom loved and cared about. I knew this was exactly how she would have wanted to pass. As I was surveying the room, I noticed a face I did not recognize. Apparently she was a pastor and a family friend of some sorts. By this time my mom began rolling in her bed because the pain was so unbearable; her face was tense and I could tell she longed to take her seat in paradise. I watched intently as she looked at us all one last time and then closed her eyes forever.

Immediately after that I noticed a light shining on her face and the most beautiful smile illuminated across her face. This was amazing because my mom had not smiled in a long time. Then I heard a voice in the back of the room say something I will never forget. "You see that smile? Your mom just saw Jesus." I looked around to see who echoed those simple yet profound words. There she was, the pastor lady (I still have no idea who she was). Her words were so confident; like she had seen this countless times before. I don't know if this lady was real or if God decided to send an angel to help comfort my family in our time of grief, but I know this woman was a gift from God.

I had never seen death before and it was nothing like I expected. Although I was filled with pain and grief and devastated by the loss of one of my best friends, a part of me was excited for my mom to go to heaven. I know that my mom believed in Jesus and it was her time to go. Over the next few months, I spent a lot of time evaluating my life and how far I have come with my walk with Christ. It was during this painful time in my life that I came to one of the clearest revelations of my entire life. I was thinking back on my old life and how different things could have been if I never got into my accident. I thought about what I might be doing or where I might have lived. During one service I heard a pastor talking about the possessions and values we hold strong to that keep us away from fully embracing God. I listened as this pastor talked about his love for deer hunting. He told us that when he wasn't doing church stuff, he spent a lot of time in the woods. He spoke on how hunting was taking time away from his Bible reading, discipling, and time with his family. He knew he had become a "slave to hunting." Then he challenged us; he asked us to examine our own lives and see what was holding us captive and what we were slaves to. It was at that point that it clicked: I thought back to my basketball days and how much time I spent playing. Basketball was always first in my life and I didn't have room for much of anything else. Then I thought back to my "desperate prayer" (the one where I gave permission to God to make a change in my life "by any means necessary.") I realized that my accident was the answer to my prayer. God knew that as long as basketball was part of my life, there would never be any room for Him. God knew that in order for me to be fully who He created me to be, I needed to die to my old self and be rebuilt from the ground up.

Jeremiah 29:11–13: "For I know the plans I have for you, declares the Lord, plans to prosper you and not to harm you, plans to give you hope and a future. Then you will call upon me and come and pray to me, and I will listen to you. You will seek me and find me when you seek me with all your heart."

Chapter Thirteen

THIS CRAZY GUY NAMED JASON

N ow that I was starting to realize what a "gift" my accident really was, I wanted to know more. I needed to bring my relationship with Christ up another level. I was doing everything I thought a Christian was supposed to be doing: I was praying, reading my Bible, volunteering my time, and going to church. What else could there be? One Sunday morning at Rivertree, I heard a young pastor named Jason speak. I could tell how much he loved Jesus by his passion and enthusiasm. He spoke about the importance of relationships and community. He went on to say that we were created to be in relationship with other believers. He told us how community is such a vital part of one's spiritual growth. As I was digesting what this man was saying, I realized that besides my wife I didn't really have any other Christians in my life. I didn't have anybody to hold me accountable, nobody to challenge me, and nobody to help me grow. As I listened to Jason speak, he gave examples from the Bible about relationships and not trying to do it alone. He taught us about Jesus sending out the disciples two by two. He referenced Mark 16 and the Great Commission. As I was sitting there

I became excited. This is what I needed. I had to get out of my comfort zone, find a solid community of friends, and start entering into relationships with nonbelievers.

As Jason was finishing up his sermon, he said if anyone wanted to know more about "community" to get a hold of him and he would love to talk. Then he proceeded to do something that made me want to follow him even more. He challenged us on what we thought was important. He asked if we would be willing to give anything we had to help a brother or sister in need. Then he threw out a challenge to the congregation: he asked us if we would be willing to give up the shoes on our feet to help people in need (literally). There were boxes placed at all the exits of the church where we could drop off our shoes and pick up a pair of plastic slippers to walk home. I looked at my shoes and remembered I was wearing my favorite pair — my brand-new blue sneakers that my mother-in-law bought me for Christmas. I thought about it for a minute, *Man, I really don't want to give these shoes away*. As much as I wanted to sneak out the back door and keep my shoes for myself, I knew I couldn't do it. Something deep inside of me was telling me it was time. So I walked to the exit, took off my shoes, and dropped them into the box.

As I drove home from church that Sunday, I became more and more intrigued with what I heard that day. I wanted to know more. I decided to reach out to Jason and see if he would be willing to meet with me sometime that week. So I sent him an email and he responded back. We decided to meet at a local coffee shop on a Monday evening. He told me to be there at 7:00 and to bring a Bible. I wasn't sure what to expect; I had never hung around any religious people before, let alone a pastor. I arrived early and got my wheelchair out of the backseat of my car. As I rolled in I thought to myself, *Wow, these are two things I never thought I would be doing — meeting with a pastor and going to a trendy coffee shop*. I spotted Jason and rolled right up to him. I wondered what he was thinking as I made my way through the crowds over to his table. When I sent him the email, I never told him I was in a chair. He gave me a big smile and shook my hand. This was the beginning of our amazing ministry together. After a few minutes of talking, Jason asked me why I wanted to meet with him. I told him I was really intrigued by what he said about "relational community" and I wanted to obtain a better understanding of the scriptures. "Okay, he said, did you bring your Bible?" I took out this pink and purple Study Bible that a girl I had dated gave me a few years earlier. He commented on my "pretty purple Bible" and still to this day has not let me live it down.

Jason really knows the Bible and I was having trouble staying with him. He was jumping from verse to verse and asking what I thought about it. I usually gave the same lame answer every time he asked me, something like, "Um, I think Paul is saying this to get us to love God more!" I had no clue what I was talking about. Thank God Jason had patience with me and didn't just push my chair out in front of a moving vehicle out of frustration. I remember trying to find the different books of the Bible. Jason would ask me to find a verse in Matthew, then Ephesians, then Isaiah—I had no idea if we were in the New Testament or the Old Testament! Usually I would have to refer back to the index to find out where in the world were all these different books. After we studied a verse of scripture or a topic for a while, Jason would always ask me one or both of these questions: "What does this verse mean to you," or "What is this verse saying to you?" This was my first opportunity to reflect on God's word and listen to what Jesus was saying to me. I was using that pretty pink Bible all the time. Jason kept telling me to "stay in the word," eventually things will start to come together. Slowly I started to understand. I started to recognize the names of these important people I kept hearing about in church. After a month or so of meeting, I didn't have to go to the index as much, I knew where Mathew, Mark, Luke, and John were located.

After meeting with Jason for a while he approached me with an idea. He asked me what I thought of inviting a few more guys to join us in our study. I have to admit at first I was selfish. I thought, *No way! I'm just now learning this Bible stuff and now you want to bring in more men.* I still didn't understand the concept of *community.* All I thought was there would be more people, so Jason would have less time to focus on me and all of my needs (I was still a selfish punk!). After some encouraging, I agreed to start meeting with these new men.

After my Monday night meetings with Jason, he often asked me if I wanted to go with him to something called "Streetlights." It was a dinner–Bible study–hangout time with a group of men in downtown Canton that I really wanted nothing to do with—the homeless. Every Monday Jason would go and pour into these men's lives. Every time he asked me I had some excuse ready to go. One night when I was all out of excuses I agreed to go. Now I had been to Canton before, but being the small-town guy I was, I tried to not make it a habit. I was convinced I was going to either get stabbed, shot, or robbed. As I walked into this run-down building in the streets of Canton, it was nothing like I expected. I was greeted with many smiling faces, and some homeless guy asked me if I wanted a hotdog. Everyone seemed to be in a good mood. Some were playing corn hole, some were playing cards, and others were outside talking. I walked in and took a seat in the metal chair closest to the door. I looked around for Jason but he was nowhere to be found. I tried to act cool, like being in a homeless shelter didn't faze me one bit, but I'm pretty sure the guys could tell I was nervous. One man sat down next to me and then another. They wanted to know who I was and what I was doing down there. Then they started to tell me some of their stories and backgrounds. It was fascinating to hear what some of these men had been through in their lives. Before my trip down to the Refuge of Hope (that was the name of the shelter,) I was one of those people who thought all homeless people were either on drugs, criminals, or too stinking lazy to get a job. The more I talked to these men, the more God began to break down the walls I had built up around my heart. By the end of the night I was having such a blast that I didn't want to leave. Over the next six months we spent a lot of time down there. I witnessed transformations beyond my imagination. I witnessed men getting baptized, being healed, and multiple individuals coming to Christ. There is something special about that place; it seems like every time we went there God was doing something amazing. One of my favorite memories was one where I got the honor of leading a broken and hurting man back to Christ. It happened when a few of us had gathered outside during a prayer event. We set up a cross and asked every one there to take a piece of paper and write down a sin in their lives that was "holding them captive" right now. Then we had them take a nail and hammer it into this large 8-foot wooden cross set up outside. After my group finished up, a man came up to me and asked me how he could restore his relationship with Jesus. I was scared out of my mind. I had never had a conversation like this before. I tried my hardest to think back to all the times I watched Jason do this in the past. He made it seem so simple, the words easily flowing so eloquently. I searched for the right type of "Jesus words" and just said, "Let 'er rip!" I told the man to close his eyes. I told him to imagine he was sitting at the foot of the cross staring at Jesus. I asked him a few questions, "Do you believe that Jesus died for your sins? Do you believe that Jesus concurred death and rose from the grave? Are you ready to surrender your life fully to Christ?" Then I asked the man to imagine all the sins he has ever committed going through his body up into the broken and bloody body of Jesus Christ. After I finished, we hugged this man. Now, I'm not a pastor and I don't know if that's the right way to lead a person back into the presence of God or not, but I felt like that's what the Holy Spirit was leading me to do and say that night. Although it was the homeless man who came to Christ that night—I felt different, like God had done some transformation in my life. And this is just the type of events that we came to expect on our journeys to downtown

Canton. The Refuge of Hope became a regular part of our Monday and Thursday night Bible studies.

During our time at the Refuge of Hope, I started meeting with a group of men once a week to study scripture. We met at parks, churches, and people's homes. We had guys from all different backgrounds and were at different places in their "walks with Christ." One of my favorite people in this group was a high-ranking ex-gang member who I will call "M." The first time I met this man was at his home. His home was not located in the safest section of town. As I walked into his home for the first time, I was greeted by his lovely wife and awesome kids. This family was amazing! As we began our study, we introduced ourselves and gave a brief testimony of who we were and who we got to this point with God. As I listened to the stories, I was blown away by what Jesus was doing in each of our lives. Each of us came to Christ in a different way, but the Holy Spirit was at work in us all the same way. I thought how crazy this was that a group of people so completely different could come together for the same reason—Jesus. As the months went on we would call each other or send texts just to see how everyone was doing. We would pray together, serve together, and fellowship together. For the first time in my life I was experiencing real "Christian Community" and I loved it!

Chapter Fourteen

A MIRACLE
NAMED KAYMEN

One of the many things that stink about living as a quadriplegic is that it's not just the external part of your body that's paralyzed (i.e. your arms and legs), but you also have to deal with internal issues as well. The absolute worst part of that for me is my bladder (every quad has their preference). Because of the level and severity of my injury, I have what is called a neurogenic bladder. It's basically just a fancy word for "you pee on yourself a lot bladder." My muscles that hold the urine are not strong enough to do their job, so when I have the urge to use the restroom, I have a 2–3 minute window to find a bathroom before it's too late. I have experienced the humiliation of peeing on myself many times. Since my injury thirteen years ago, I have become an expert at urinating in empty bottles and finding places along busy roads. Like I said, I hate it. Right next to my bladder, without going into too much detail, the next thing I despise the most about being a quadriplegic is the issues that come along with my "man parts." This is usually issue *numero uno* for any spinal cord patient over sixteen and under sixty years old. This was no different for me.

After I got married and found out I was still in working condition, my wife and I decided we wanted to try and have a baby. Suzie and I were trying for a few months when we got the good news. I remember running to a store at midnight just to double-check the test to make sure it was accurate. I was so excited to be a daddy and couldn't believe God wanted to entrust me with one of His children. After twenty weeks, Suzie went to the doctor's to read the ultrasound and find out if it was a boy or a girl. Suzie really wanted a little girl (in fact, I think she painted the room purple before the ultrasound visit), but I could care less as long as it was healthy. We waited anxiously as the nurse examined this precious child. Then she said the words my wife was aching to hear, "Well, it looks like a girl."

Finally after nine long months, our baby girl was born. We decided on the name Kaymen (yes like the island and the crocodile). I couldn't believe I was a daddy. I remember staring at this little girl in the hospital and being so amazed at God's creation. I had no idea what I was doing. I had never changed a diaper, never fed a baby, and I've only actually held an infant a couple of times in my life. The nurses at the hospital were used to dads like me. They didn't cut me any slack—they threw me right into it. After a few days and a many busted diapers, I finally got the hang of it. Before we left the hospital, we had to take a mini class on how to care for babies at home. They wanted to make sure we could take care of these little people when we got home. I enjoyed watching all the other dads struggle (like myself) at simple tasks like giving our kids baths or putting on their tiny little outfits.

A few days later it was time to take Kaymen home. We loaded her into her new car seat and started out towards the expressway. I don't think I ever broke 45 miles per hour on that drive home. I obeyed every traffic law (for the first time in my life) and was screaming at all the other obnoxious drivers who were going too fast. Once we got Kaymen home, I put her in her little basinet on the kitchen table and Suzie and I began to cry. We wondered how in the world we were going to take care of this little fragile infant. It was easy at the hospital: if we needed anything, the nurses would take care of it; now it was all on us. After a few weeks I got the hang of it. Her feeding schedule was like clockwork. She would wake up two to three times a night, with my wife and me taking turns grabbing a bottle. I always volunteered to do the 2:00 AM feeding because the sports report was on and I could catch up on all the days's scores. I loved those nights; Kaymen's little eyes would stare at the TV and try to become mesmerized by all the colors and noises the television would produce. Sometimes when Kaymen would curl up on my chest after those feedings, I had time to reflect on how lucky I was and how cool it was that I served such an amazing God who would allow me to enjoy this amazing treasure.

As my daughter continued to grow, I began to realize how important it was for her to grow up knowing Jesus. I was spending a lot of time at the homeless shelter and in different Bible studies. I was making intentional time to invest in men's lives and trying to make disciples as best I knew how, but it was taking a toll on my family. I was working full time and spending my nights doing ministry. After a few years of this, I realized that although it was great that I was spending so much time doing different types of ministries, I was failing miserably at making disciples in my own home. My wife and I were too busy to read scripture or even pray together before we went to bed. I examined my life and knew that I had to make a change; I had to find a healthy balance. I decided to cut back on some of my obligations and spend more time with my family. Instead of studying the scriptures with total strangers on the street, we studied God's word as a family. We spent time praying together before we went to sleep. This was an important step in my life and probably saved my marriage.

During this time in my life, I really started to miss basketball. It was always such a huge part of my life and it was killing me to know that I would never play again. I was also sad because I had this brand-new little girl who would only know her dad as that guy who limps around everywhere. It made me upset to know that I would not be able to teach her how to ride a bike, coach her softball team, or even just run in the backyard with her. I became angry—I know I was lucky to be able to walk and a lot of people would change places with me in a second, but I was still mad. It's funny: at my million different basketball practices I've had in my life, the thing I hated most was running sprints. I used to yell and complain when my coach would put us on the line to run. Now thirteen years later I would kill to have the opportunity to run just one more lap. I missed it—I missed everything about athletics. I needed to fill that empty void in my life that basketball used to occupy.

While I was in the hospital, my therapists used to tell me about wheelchair sports. They would tell me how cool those were and they even had an Olympics for them. Me being the arrogant twenty-one-year-old wanted nothing to do with them. I thought it was lame. I thought, *How tough can wheelchair sports really be?* I wanted nothing to do with them at the time, but now that I knew I would be paralyzed the rest of my life, it may be worth looking into. I started researching the different sports that were available for people in wheelchairs. I was looking for something extreme, like boxing or football. I was never interested in wheelchair basketball because it would be too hard for me to get back on a basketball court, plus my triceps were paralyzed and I couldn't get the stupid ball up to the hoop. One day I came across a sport that I never heard of that had the right mixture of athleticism and extreme craziness I was searching for. It was a relatively new sport called wheelchair rugby, or more affectionately named "murderball." It is a mixture of football and basketball with a hint of racing thrown in there. It is played on a basketball court and there are four players on each team. The goal is to get the ball into your opponent's goal. It sounds easy but there is a lot of strategy that goes along with it. When a player has the ball, he is only allowed to possess it for five seconds before they have to dribble it. The other players on the team set picks and try to help move the ball into the goal. The defensive team does whatever they can to stop the ball from crossing the goal line (similar to football). While I was reading about it online it seemed pretty tame, but then I went to my first practice and experienced "murderball" live in action. First off, these are not your average everyday hospital wheelchairs. They look like miniature little tanks. The first time I got into one I was amazed at how light and easy to push they were. Next, I learned there was a reason for the crazy design of these chairs—people hit you with them, HARD. I was not expecting paralyzed quadriplegics to hit with the ferocity that they do. It is not uncommon to see a player fall out of there chair onto the hard floor. Then instead of being compassionate, the other players look at you and tell you to "get your worthless self up" and start playing again. It was brutal, it was bloody, it was extreme, and it was exactly what I needed!

Stretching out with Kaymen before a murderball game.

Because I did not spend all of my time in a chair, I was one of the slowest players on our team. The guys on my team gave me the nickname "Legs" because I could walk, kind of. I watched as the other players raced up and down the court as I struggled to keep up. I still remember that "jarring" feeling I would get when one of the players would come at me full speed and crash into me. My body would tense up and it felt like a semitruck just ran over me. Although I was not very fast or strong, I did have one thing going for me— basketball. From all the years of playing ball, I was able to use some of those skills on the rugby court. For instance, I was able to get open all the time. When the defensive team saw the ball crossing half-court, they immediately took off to try and stop the ball. Well, when I saw my guy leave to help, I took off the other way and was usually wide open. I also was good at reading defenses. In basketball I had to know if the defensive team was running a "zone" or a "man" defense. It was the same concept in rugby. Once I determined what the other team was doing defensively, I quickly scanned the court and was able to find the open man for the easy goal.

Murderball was exactly what I needed. Although I was not very good, it felt great to be playing a sport again. As much as I loved to be competing again, one of the things I loved most about my time playing rugby was my team. We traveled on the weekends to different states and got to bring our families along to watch us play. I loved staying at the hotels and learning more about my teammates and their families. Each one of us had a different story and had unique obstacles that we dealt with on a daily basis. These serve as therapeutic times for our wives as well because they could talk to each other and vent about their frustrations that stem from marrying a quadriplegic. I loved to sit around the pool after the games and enjoy a drink or two with my new friends. The problem for me was that one drink typically turned into five drinks and then shots of liquor would soon follow. It seemed innocent enough; I would catch a buzz, hang out with my boys, and then head back to my family who were sleeping back in the room. My friends used to think it was funny when I would get out of my chair after a few drinks. It was a struggle for me to walk sober; add some alcohol to it and I was falling down all over the place. They thought it was hilarious. Then after a few tournaments, I no longer was drinking just to catch a buzz, now I was drinking to get hammered. I would even start drinking during the games. If we had a break between games, I would sneak out to the car or into the bathroom and do a couple shots of vodka. I didn't think it was a big deal at all. I was always one of the first people at the early morning games. I was never late and the heavy drinking didn't seem to be affecting my game any way. In fact I think I was actually playing better when I had a few drinks in me. I convinced myself that this was all just innocent fun and I deserved to do this because my life sucked and I was paralyzed. Besides, I still had an amazing relationship with Jesus, I was going to church, leading Bible studies, discipling people, and bringing people to Christ. I should be able to have a little fun on the weekends, right?

The funny thing about developing a relationship with God is what He starts doing inside of your heart. Once you give your life to Christ, you are no longer the same person. I knew what I was doing was not glorifying Christ and He was letting me know it. I felt myself slipping back into my old ways and God was putting the brakes on it. It took a few years but I realized that if I was going to follow Jesus, I couldn't do it halfway. Although I loved my rugby friends and my time playing murderball, I knew I needed to stop. I was not strong enough to just "hang out" on the weekends. I gave the Devil a foothold and he ran with it. I decided it was time to get my life back in order and give Jesus back that part of my heart I was trying to keep for myself.

Chapter Fifteen

LET'S GO TO PERU

Over the next two years I committed to strengthening my relationship with Christ. I treated this time just as I did when I was training for athletics. I spent time in the word. I spent time in prayer. I looked to surround myself with other men with who loved Jesus and help me stay on the right path. It was during this time that I experienced a great spiritual healing. I had no idea that I was about to experience a physical healing as well.

During one of my weekly meetings with Jason, we got on the subject of spiritual gifts. He asked me what I thought my gift was. Of course still relatively young in my walk, I had no idea what my spiritual gift was. I doubted if I even had any gift at all. Then he started to talk about the gift of healing. He told me about this pastor friend he had that had a religious organization in downtown Canton. He went on to tell me that this man has healed a lot of people on a fairly regular basis. I was intrigued but very skeptical. It sounded like voodoo and rattlesnake handling to me. After going home that night, I started to think about the Bible and all the people who Jesus and the disciples healed. I started thinking that maybe there really was something to this healing stuff and if Jason knew this guy, he must be legit. So at our next meeting, I asked Jason if he would introduce me to this man and maybe he could try and heal me. So Jason contacted his friend and he agreed to meet me.

The next part of my story doesn't seem real. Even as I'm writing this down, I can't believe the series of events that unfolded. Here goes....

We decided to meet at a small local Christian music television station. This pastor was doing a half-hour sermon during the television station's telethon program. I walked into this place and was completely overwhelmed by how nice everybody was. I was a total stranger to these people, but they were giving us the grand tour of the building and offering us an amazing dinner they had prepared. As I walked into the television studio, I couldn't help but notice how bright everything was. It felt like a tanning bed in there. I watched as the husband and wife who ran the TV ministry pleaded with the audience to help support the ministry. There were songs, testimonies, and stories about Jesus. Everybody in there looked like they were over the age of sixty-five. It was exactly like what you see when you come across one of those religious programs on cable TV. Everyone was dressed like they were going to their senior prom. The women all had different bright colors of extremely large hairdos. The men were decked out in suits and ties. Everybody was happy and kept saying things like, "Praise Jesus!" every other sentence. These people loved Jesus—I mean really loved Jesus. At one point I got so caught up in the experience that I just wrote a check out for fifty dollars and gave it to some random person. I was fascinated by what I was witnessing and couldn't take my eyes off this production. Once I gathered my thoughts, I turned to my left to find my friend Jason was gone. I searched the building and finally found him alone in the dinner room with a piece of fried chicken in his mouth.

After the show was over and Jason and I finished scarfing down the free food, I met the pastor. He was nothing like I expected. He was a little man and had to be around eighty years old. Of all the places we could have met, we were introduced in a big coat room.

He greeted me with a smile, and Jason filled him in on my physical condition. At this point I had absolutely no idea what to expect. Keeping with the theme of the night, I was fully prepared for this man to slap me in the head and say, "You're healed!" or maybe throw some Holy Water on me or something. To my surprise, this kind, gentle old man had me sit in a chair, laid his hands on me, and prayed. He prayed like he wasn't asking Jesus to heal me—he expected Jesus to heal me. As soon as he finished praying, I looked around to see what was going to happen next. Was this going to be like one of the healings in the Bible wherein the paralyzed person jumps up and starts running around the room? I stood up out of the chair and felt this strange electrical shock type sensation pulsate through my legs. At first I didn't notice a change (awkward!). Then I took a step—wow that felt good! Then I took another...and another. One of the effects of a spinal cord injury is muscle spasms and tone. They make my legs extremely stiff (like a guitar string) and difficult to move. This muscle issue is a constant problem that I deal with on a daily basis. Anyways, what I noticed is after the prayer, the tone and the spasms were gone. I could walk around the room with no pain and virtually no limp at all. I looked at this man to thank him and he didn't look impressed by this at all. He just smiled and put his coat on and walked out the door. It was like he expected a miracle to occur.

As the night went on, I became more and more overjoyed. I came into this building "limping" and went out of it "walking." I was so filled with the Holy Spirit that I didn't know what to do. I remember pulling into different driveways in the city of Canton just to pray. I prayed like I have never prayed before. I prayed "earnestly," whatever that means. I thanked God for this miracle and for all He has done in my life. I'm not sure what praying in tongues is all about, but this was about as close to that as I have ever experienced. I remember walking down the streets of Canton that night overwhelmed with joy. I didn't want the night to end because I feared I would get up the next morning and it would all be gone.

The next day I narrated all the events of the previous night to my wife as I was sitting on the floor. For the last seven years of physical therapy, one of the things they were working with me on was to be able to get off the floor without grabbing onto something for support. The only way I could do it was to use a table or couch and pull my body up using my arms. I must have tried that a hundred times during therapy and failed miserably each time. Since I was already sitting on the ground, I decided to give it a shot. I sat up on my knees and pushed up—before I knew it, I was standing up. *That had to be a fluke*, I thought to myself, *just leftover adrenaline from last night.* So I tried it again—same result. Tried it another time, I came right off the floor and stood up. Now I know to the average person this may not seem like a big deal, but to a quadriplegic seven years after their accident it's huge—it's a miracle!

I believe what God was doing that night was demonstrating His power. If He wanted to, He could have healed me completely right there on the spot. Instead, I believe God chose to reveal to me just a tiny glimpse of what He could do. I also believe God knew I needed this injury. He knew I needed this paralysis. It is my story—my way of connecting with people. It's my way of showing people how God can take a desperate broken man and use them to do extraordinary things. My accident is a gift! I often tell people if I could go back in time and have the option of never being paralyzed, I wouldn't do it.

2 Corinthians 12:7: "To keep me from becoming conceited because of these surpassingly great revelations, there was given me a thorn in my flesh."

To me, battling quadriplegia on a daily basis is the "thorn in my flesh."

After an experience like that, I was left with the question of "Now, what?" This is essentially the second time that God has done a significant healing in my life—what was I doing in return? One evening while I was sitting at Jason's house reflecting on all the cool stuff that God had done in our lives, it came to us—a climb. Not just any climb—a mountain climb! What better way to glorify God and all the healing He has done in my life than a crazy adventure like this. After a week of brainstorming, we decided our mountain adventure would take place in Peru climbing Machu Picchu. I had never done anything like this before, so I had no idea how to even plan a trip like this. The first thing I had to do was convince my doctor that it was a good idea for a quadriplegic with significant paralysis and extensive health issues to travel to a Third World country and climb a 12,000-foot mountain. I remember sitting in my physician's office explaining what I was about to do. He had this look on his face like I was completely insane and this was all a big joke. Once he knew I was serious, his response to my request went something like this, "Well, it was nice knowing you, Brian." It's funny that as I continued to tell people about this climb, I continued to get the response often. After a little convincing, my doctor agreed to let me go but made sure I took every possible antibiotic with me. No matter what "weird" illness I may contract in Peru—I was covered. Now that I had my doctor's blessing, I had to make sure that my body was physically able to handle the rigorous pounding that climbing a mountain would entail.

I started a workout program at my house and was stretching my body as close to its limit as possible. I would wake early in the morning and try to get a few miles in before work. I walked a 5K with the four other men who were going on the trip with me. I did anything I could to prepare my body for the climb. We decided that not only were we going to climb this mountain as a celebration of what God has done in my life, we also were going to document the entire trip and try to raise funds for a global ministry organization. So along with training for the climb, I was busy talking to corporate sponsors and trying to convince them to donate to this worthy cause. I was blown away by the amount of support I received from family, friends, and donors. As the trip was getting closer, we asked a professional cinematographer to accompany us on our trip and make the film. He started filming the entire process up until we boarded the plane. At times I felt like I was in a reality TV show because I was always hooked up to a microphone or had a camera in my face. About a week before we were scheduled to leave, I had an entire camera crew at my home filming the last segment before we left for Peru. We had everything set, everything booked, and everything was in place.

During this final interview, I turned on the television in the bedroom and couldn't believe what I was hearing: the airline we bought our tickets through had just announced they were going on strike and cancelling all flights until a resolution was found. I was devastated. I wanted to go on this trip badly. And to make matters worse, I had corporate investors who donated money to our trip. It was a helpless feeling; my team and I tried everything we could to get another flight, but they were all booking up fast. My wife and I were up at 3:00 AM trying to find any airline that could get us to Lima. We looked at driving to Washington, DC, Philadelphia, and Detroit, any airport that had an international hub. We couldn't find anything; and the flights we could find were three times as expensive as what we paid for our tickets. It was looking more and more like we were going to have to cancel our trip. We continued to hold out for any type of miracle to come our way. Then we got a glimpse of hope from an unusual source.

Two days before we were scheduled to arrive in Peru, I decided to go "Rambo Style" and make one last effort to will this trip into happening. I started calling anybody and everybody I could find and see if they could help us. Somehow I came across a phone number for a maintenance person at the Cleveland Airport. I don't know why I thought a janitor could help us out but hey, I was desperate. I called this man but he was not there. I left some two-minute babbling incoherent message about what was going on and pleading for some help. To my surprise, he called me back and gave me the phone number of a contact he had with Continental Airlines. It turned out this was not some ordinary contact; she was a high executive in the Northeast Region. I called this woman and told her what was going on. She was amazing! She was able to calm me down and told me she would see what she could do to help.

Later on that day I got some more unexpected assistance. I reached out to the Public Relations department at Metro Health Medical Center in Cleveland and asked if they could help. She contacted her friend at a major Cleveland news channel, and they sent someone over to my house that night. They interviewed me and gave me the opportunity to tell my story to hundreds of thousands of people. I told them about why I was doing this trip and the amazing ministry that we were trying to raise money for. It was absolutely remarkable to see how God was working through this process. Earlier in the day I was ready to cancel the trip and now I was getting to promote it on television. God was doing His thing and I just needed to get out of the way and allow it to happen.

As I went to bed that night, I was reflecting on everything that had taken place that day. I was ecstatic that God was placing these awesome people in my life, but we were scheduled to be in Peru in 24 hours and had nothing in place. As I fell asleep that night, I asked God for help. We needed a hero. We needed someone to step outside of themselves and come to our rescue. I knew this was a long shot, but I continued to hold on to hope; hope that God would provide a way for us to go on this journey.

The next day I spent a lot of time on the phone. Continental Airlines called me in the morning and informed me they were working on a solution to get us on a plane. I had people calling me all day giving us support and praying for us. I had total strangers call me at home and offer us their Frequent Flyer miles. I had people calling and wanting to know about my injury and what medical devices I was using on the trip. The outpouring of support was unbelievable. As the day went on I became more and more stressed. I began to watch the clock as the minutes continued to tick away. It was now 3:30 PM Tuesday afternoon—we were scheduled to leave for Peru 6:00 AM the next day—and we still had no plane tickets. At 3:45 I got the call I had been dreaming about. Before I knew it I was on a conference call with the executives from Continental Airlines in Cleveland and Houston. These people were so amazing! They told me Continental decided to put us on a plane the next morning—and it was going to be cheaper than our original price. They told me if I had booked five tickets with them that day for Lima, Peru, it would have cost around $15,000. They gave us the tickets for less than $3,000!

The next day we left for Cleveland early in the morning. Because of everything going on the past week, I really didn't have time to emotionally prepare myself to leave my family. I know it was only a weeklong trip, but I had never left my wife and baby for more than a weekend. I remember before I left that day I wrote them a letter and told them how much I loved them and would miss them. Once we got to the airport, we were met by a local news crew who wanted to get a shot of us boarding the plane. We must have looked like rock stars because everyone was looking at us wondering why a camera crew was following us around. As we got to the ticket counter, we were greeted by an extremely friendly Continental staff. They recognized me from the news last night and seemed really excited to help us out. A few minutes later, a woman named Monika appeared with our tickets. I like to think that Monika is "my angel" sent straight from Christ himself. She was the contact person from Continental who made everything possible for us to go. After we got our tickets, we were ushered to the VIP portion of the check-in and got to go to the front of the line. After we made it through security, Monika arranged for a golf cart to pick us up and take us to our plane. Once we boarded the plane, I felt a huge sense of relief. Our seats were awesome! We were sitting in the first row so I had plenty of leg room to stretch out during the long flight to Houston. Right before the flight was about to take off, I saw Monika board the plane. She gave us all passes to the Continental Club in Houston. The Continental Club is this really cool place for frequent travelers to relax with free food, drinks, showers, and really comfortable couches. I could not believe the generosity Continental was showing us. I was very emotional and had trouble containing myself. As Monika left the plane, she gave us all a hug and wished us well on our trip. I will never forget Monika—I needed a hero and got an ANGEL!

Finally our plane touched down in Lima, Peru, around 11:30 PM that night. I have never traveled to a place like Lima before, so I had no idea what to expect. As soon as I stepped off the plane and entered the lobby, I knew I wasn't in the States anymore. The first thing I noticed was people everywhere yelling and screaming—in Spanish. I was fascinated by the sheer number of people who were held back by nothing more than a rope. I remember it being really bright in the airport; it reminded me of being in Vegas. I had no idea what time of day it was. Lucky for us one of the men on our trip had connections in Peru and made arrangements for someone to pick us up at the airport. The man who picked us up was named "Ricky." He was our guide for the week. When I tell people about our trip, I often tell them if we didn't have Ricky, I'm pretty sure we would have died on multiple occasions. As we loaded our bags into Ricky's tiny yellow van, I had an opportunity to look around the area. It was beautiful, not at all like I had expected. As we pulled away from the airport and headed to our Hostel in Chillica, I started to see my first signs of an "impoverished community." We stopped at a gas station and bought bottled water to use for the week. The tap water in the area was contaminated, and if you ingested it you will get extremely sick. We had to brush our teeth with bottled water and make sure we kept our mouth closed as we were taking showers.

After we got to the hostel and checked in, it was rally late. I sat outside for a while and looked at the ocean. This is the first time I had ever seen the Pacific Ocean and it was beautiful. We arrived in Peru in June, which is their winter time (if you call 65 degrees winter). I stared out onto the beach and imagined what it would look like during summer. I wondered if the local kids would be building sand castles while their parents were sitting under umbrellas. The next morning I woke up early and walked down onto the cool sand. I watched as the local children walked up and down the beach on their way to school. They could tell I wasn't from around there; they would look at me cautiously then start to giggle with their friends. This was quite different from back home. I wondered where these kids' parents were and why they were letting them walk down a public beach alone. I didn't know at the time, but a lot of these kids didn't even have parents, let alone someone responsible enough to take care of them. I walked around the side of the building to the front entrance. I looked around and everything looked dirty and run-down. There were no nice buildings or shiny cars. There were no big homes, and people were not dressed in fancy clothes. The people were very friendly. Most of them would smile or wave at me as I passed by. I wish I would have taken the time to learn Spanish before coming, because communication became a big deficiency.

Standing in front of Hannah's Home in Chilca, Peru.

Finally the rest of the guys woke up and we had breakfast. We talked about our day and what we would be doing the rest of the week. Our first day we would be visiting a place called Hannah's Home. It was a safe place for young girls who had babies or were currently pregnant. I was excited to visit this place because I had heard the pastor of my church talk about all the cool things going on there. As we started the 20-minute drive, I got the chance to look at this community during the day. I was blown away by what I saw. The living conditions that these Peruvians were living in bordered on inhumane. Their homes were made of old car doors or pieces of tin. The floors were all made of dirt or mud and there was no indoor toilet. I also noticed that these homes often connected with other ones. I was later informed that these structures were called "squatter villages." It was not uncommon to have a family of five living in a one-room 8 by 8-foot shack. I tried to prepare myself to see this type of poverty, but I was not prepared for it to be so severe. It invoked all kinds of emotion within me: anger, sadness, guilt, and disappointment.

A typical squatter home in the coastal town of Chilca, Peru.

Once we got to the facility, my mood and spirits began to be lifted. I got to meet some of these amazing people and I was blown away by their positive attitudes. Even though they were living in what I would call "deplorable" conditions, they were some of the happiest people I have ever met. It didn't matter to them what their homes looked like or how much money they had, they were just happy to be alive. It was almost as though they didn't even know they were living in poverty. As I continued to tour the facility, I was seeing God at work everywhere I looked. The people at Hannah's were making such a positive impact on these young mothers and children. They were teaching them how to care for themselves and their children. They were giving them a safe place to stay and teaching them about Jesus.

After dinner they asked us if we wanted to go out into the community and help with VBS (Vacation Bible School). I had no idea what VBS was, but I was definitely up for anything at that point. We all loaded back into that tiny van and headed to the middle of this tiny village. Once we got there, I noticed we were the only ones there. It was so quiet; no one was around and it looked like all the homes were abandoned. Then the volunteers got out their microphone and started to sing. Before I knew it, there were kids coming at us from every direction. It was as if every home had ten kids living inside of it. As the kids all gathered in the middle of the sports complex, I watched as the four other men I was with each grabbed a handful of kids and started playing with them. I stood there like a statue. I didn't know what to do. I couldn't participate in most of the activities because of my paralysis. I was sad as I watched everyone having a great time. Then a few children came and stood around me. I smiled at them. I knew they wanted me to play with them but I couldn't. After a few awkward moments, I had an idea. To help me walk better during my trip, I was fitted with an electronic walking device that was powered by batteries. Every time I bent my knee, it kicked my leg up and helped me push my leg through. I pulled my pant leg up and showed a couple kids how it worked.

They pushed the button and watched my leg jump. They laughed and wanted to do it again. I told them it was okay and they pushed it again—my leg jumped again! By this time each kid had called their friends over and before I knew it I was surrounded by children pushing their way up to me to get a chance to press the button. This was it—although I couldn't run or jump with them, my injury was giving me the opportunity to have this amazing interaction with these precious children. For the next two hours we sang, danced, and played with these amazing children. When it was time for us to leave they did not want us to go. They all surrounded our vans and raised their tiny little hands up towards the window hoping that we would grab on to them for one last shake. I was sad—I did not want to leave, but I realized this was just the beginning of our journey—Jesus had much more in store for us to accomplish!

Playing with the local children during Vacation Bible School.
Love these kids!

A few days later we boarded a plane and flew to Cusco, Peru. Cusco was about an hour away from Lima. We flew through some of the most beautiful mountain ranges I had ever seen. I knew the altitude was going to be a challenge for me, so I prepared myself as best as I could. When we landed I felt good. My head was a little dizzy, but other than that I was good. We jumped into our cab and headed for our hotel. I feel in love with this tiny city as soon as we got there. We arrived at our hotel a few minutes later. This small little hotel was nicer than many large ones I stay at here in the States. What I remember most is the craftsmanship of the wood. It was perfect. The color was a dark stain that was applied perfectly to the walls and trim. The doors were solid and wide, and they complimented the décor well. They had a quaint little lobby area and a breakfast area where they served a home-cooked meal every morning and would not let us leave until we sampled some of their fine cuisine. They also had two computers set up complete with internet access. This was a welcome sight because it allowed us access to check in with our families and gave me the opportunity to update our blog. I miss that little hotel and can't wait to go back and visit again.

After we placed our bags into the room, we decided to "hit the streets" and see what the city had to offer. About an hour into our trip to Cusco, I began to feel the effects of being over 11,000 feet in elevation. I started to get a bad headache and felt like I was going to puke. We decided the best thing to do was to grab a bit to eat and sample one of the local beers. After the meal, I felt better and that was the only effect of altitude sickness I experienced on our trip. We continued to explore the city and visited some really cool places. As we were getting ready to go back to the hotel to rest for a while, we ran into a student from a familiar place—Ohio. He was on a month trip studying and exploring some historical places in South America. He walked with us on journey back to the hotel. Once we got there, the rest of the guys went upstairs to rest. I stayed downstairs in the lobby and learned more about our new friend. Turns out he was a new dad. We talked about how difficult it was for him to be away from his wife and new baby for a month.

A few hours later my friends came back downstairs refreshed and ready to see Cusco at night. We ventured back out into the city. One off the coolest things about Cusco is the festivals. They have a parade every Saturday night and we just happened to be there in time to experience one. I watched as children sang and danced. Everywhere you looked you saw bright, beautiful and vibrant colors. After the festival I walked the streets for a couple hours visiting all the shops and street vendors. In one small shop I saw a sign that said "tattoos downstairs." Now, I love tattoos and wasn't going to pass up an opportunity to check out a tat shop in downtown Cusco. Looking back, I wouldn't advocate for anyone to go by themselves to some random tattoo parlor in the basement of a rundown vendor shop in Peru, but I was on a mission, an adventure to explore everything the city had to offer. As I started downstairs I realized I may have not made the wisest decision to venture downstairs by myself. I've been in some scary "hole in the wall" tattoo parlors in the States, but I had never seen anything like this. As I inched closer to the bottom of the stairs, the wall started to get narrower and narrower. By the time I reached the shop I looked around and quickly realized I wasn't welcome there. I waited for someone to say something but they just continued to stare at me and give me the "you better get your American self out of my shop" look. I gave it a minute because I didn't want to show these big Peruvian dudes that I was scared (kind of like when you come across a wild animal and don't want to show any fear). As soon as I had the opportunity, I bolted back up the stairs as fast as my crippled legs would carry me. Once I made it back safely to the street, we enjoyed the city for a few more hours before heading back to the hotel. We needed to get a good night's sleep because the next day was game time! It's what we flew to South America for—climbing Machu Picchu.

This would be a good time to discuss some of the physical limitations I encountered up to this point of my trip. Because of the paralysis and muscle spasms in my legs, I took six muscle relaxers a day in order for my legs to keep from stiffening up and becoming unusable. Every morning I would wake up and do a stretching routine in order to keep my body loose. This did not change just because I was in Peru. Somehow I had to find the time and space to be able to make this happen every morning. I also still had to deal with my bowel and bladder problems. Every two to three days I had to find an hour in my day to use a suppository to empty my bowels. This was extremely hard because we were on a tight schedule and finding a bathroom was not always easy. Another issue that was adding stress to my body was my lack of food consumption. I lost 15 pounds prior to this trip and lost another 5 during. I was scared to eat anything because I did know how my body was going to react, and I did not want to have to wear a diaper for the next five days. My bladder was also something I needed to be aware of. With me at all times was a backpack with all the clothes (in case of an accident) I would need, along with a urinal in case I had to pee in some random place like a plane, train, or van. I found the urinal to be extremely helpful. During one of our walks, we stopped at a roadside stand to sample a bottle of Peru's finest soda. I should have known better than to drink this particular beverage. Before we were given our drinks, I witnessed this nice lady handling raw chicken (without washing her hands) and then grabbed the bottles and told us to "enjoy." After consuming this tasty drink that had a hint of raw chicken juice on the side, I felt the urge to run to the restroom. The problem was there was not restroom to go to. After a few minutes I realized if I didn't get to the bathroom quickly I was going to pee all over my clothes. I asked our guide if I could have the keys to the van. I hurried to get the door open, and then searched my bag for my urinal. I found it and proceeded to use the front seat of Ricky's van as my own personal restroom. I repeated this about three times in the next five minutes until my body expelled all the remnants of that "tasty" cola.

Besides all the fun issues with my bowel and bladder, I had a more serious health issue that needed to be closely monitored. Because my body does not regulate temperature well (because of my accident), I am at constant risk of experiencing something called *autonomic dysreflexia*. This happens when my blood pressure gets out of control due to full bowel or bladder, infection, skin sore, ingrown toenail, tight clothing, or any painful stimulus. If not treated quickly, this can be a life-threatening ailment and lead to seizure, stroke, and even death. To protect myself, I carried a tube of nitroglycerine with me everywhere I went on the trip. I showed the guys what to do before we left in case something bad should happen to me. So you can see, it was not only being paralyzed and climbing a mountain that I had to worry about, I had real, complex medical issues that I had to manage as well.

Finally the day we had been training for had finally arrived. I was excited to get started. I remember it was the week of Father's Day so the night before our climb all the dads in the group made video messages to send to our wives and children. As we were getting our equipment loaded into the vehicle, I went and checked the computer to send an update on our blog. I checked my Facebook account and received the most amazing and encouraging letter from my wife telling me how proud she was of me. It was exactly what I needed to hear before I went and did something crazy like climb a mountain.

Just getting to the base of Machu Picchu to begin our climb was a challenge. We began our trip early in the morning with a three-hour bus trip along the beautiful Peruvian countryside. It was difficult to sleep because the motion of going up and down the hills was enough to make a person ill. About halfway to our destination, we stopped at a little convenience shack to stock up on water and snacks. I welcomed the opportunity to get out of the cramped bus and stretched my legs. At this point they were so stiff my hamstrings felt like guitar strings. After about 20 minutes we loaded back into the bus and continued on with our trip. The last 30 minutes of the bus ride was interesting. Apparently the area we were traveling had experienced some major flooding and washed away the roads. So, in order to continue on, we had to take the bus down an old set railroad tracks. It was a bumpy ride but I was glad we finally made it. The next part of our trip would take place by train. It was a two-hour ride through the Andes Mountains. I loved this ride! As we traveled along the switchbacks of the Andes, we could see little homes tucked in the side of the hills. We traveled along creek beds where anxious hikers had set up tents in anticipation of making the four-day Inca Trail climb. After five hours of traveling, we finally made it to the town of Aguas Calientes (which got its name from the hot springs located in the area). This town was at the base of Machu Picchu, and it was time to start our climb.

The first twenty minutes of our climb I was functioning on pure adrenaline. I was flying up the side of the rocky mountain. Once the excitement started to wear off, I began to hit a wall. After only 30 minutes into our climb, I was exhausted. The incline got steeper and steeper and the terrain became nearly impossible for me to traverse by myself. As much as I hated to do it, I needed to grab a hold of my friend's arms to keep from tripping and falling down the side of the mountain. We continued to push on up the side of the hill until we finally saw an opening through the trees.

It was a long hike along the trail, but we finally made it to the top.

I couldn't wait to get my first glimpse of Machu Picchu. I dragged my broken and tired body up the last few steps and hurried my way over to the clearing. As I inched closer and closer to the edge of the cliff, I got my first glimpse of how high we really were. I couldn't believe what I was actually witnessing. I had never seen such a breathtaking view in my entire life. The side of the mountain that we emerged from was higher than the ancient city of MP, so I could actually look down into the ruins. I was blown away by the craftsmanship and ingenuity of the Incan people. I couldn't understand how a city just appeared in the middle of the Andes Mountains. I wanted a closer look so I got as close to the edge as possible. My feet were literally hanging off the side of the mountain, my friends were scared to death. They kept telling me to scoot back, but I couldn't take my eyes off the amazing view.

Finally made it to the top of Machu Picchu.

After taking some video from the cliff, we started to venture down the mountain and made our way to the ruins. I don't know which was more dangerous, going up the mountain or going down it? As we hiked down the narrow pathway towards the city, the path became narrower and more unstable. As I looked over to the side, I couldn't help but think if I take one wrong step I will go hurling down 7,000 ft to the bottom of this mountain. There were no safety measures to keep people safe. No hand railings to hold on to. No ropes to keep you from getting too close to the edge. It was "climb at your own risk." All it would take was one stumble, one catch of my foot and it was over. I remember Jason saying his worst fear on the climb was the thought of having to come back to the States and tell my wife I that I fell off the side of the mountain and died!

We made it safely to the ancient city and its ruins. I walked around for a while and tried to imagine what it would have been like to live in the days of the Incans. I went in and out of old homes and admired the craftsmanship that each building exhibited. As I walked along the soft mountain grass, I encountered a stray alpaca grazing in the open. I was overcome with emotion and looked for a place to process everything I was experiencing. I went to the side of the mountain and sat down. My feet hung off the edge of the mountain and I watched the people below me as they walked along the Inca Trail. I was so high that the people looked like little ants marching in a straight line. I started to think about my life and everything I had been through. For the first time, I felt content. I was so blown away by the transformation Jesus had done in my life. As I looked around, I thought to myself, *This has to be what Heaven is like.* I was so thankful that God had heard my desperate prayers all those years ago and changed me. As I sat there inches away from death, I had a realization, "I was ready to die for the Gospel of Jesus Christ." At that moment in time I was ready to go home to be with Jesus. Someone could have come and pushed me off the side of the mountain and I would have been fine with it. Something changed in me as I sat on that ledge high in the Andes Mountains: for the first time, I no longer looked at God as just a "king" or the "creator of the universe." I saw God as my Father and Heaven as my home.

I spent a few minutes reflecting on my injury, too. I thought about how blessed I was to have the opportunity to travel to Peru and visit one of the "Wonders of the World." I realized if I was never in that car accident I may never have gotten the opportunity to do this. I thought about my friends who are still in wheelchairs who would die to have an opportunity like this. I thought about all those lonely nights I spent in my hospital bed thinking my life was over. I had come so far. My doctor called my recovery a "miracle." Looking back thirteen years later, I call it "God's plan."

As I started back down the mountain, I came across another hiker. I noticed that he was limping badly. I stopped and talked with him for a few minutes. He told me he had his leg amputated (I can't remember the reason why). I watched him as he struggled to make it up the stairs to the ruins. He carried a walking stick, but a friend was with him to help him up the mountain. I wondered why he was there. I wondered what his story was. I wondered if God had changed his life the way He changed mine.

After an exhausting day of hiking around Machu Picchu, it was time for us to climb back down the mountain. I didn't know how I was going to make it. I was so tired, my body ached, and my feet were so beat up that I could barely get one foot in front of the other. Somehow, I dragged my broken body slowly back down the mountain and to the bus waiting to pick us up. I immediately went to the back of the bus and collapsed into the seat. My heart was racing and my entire body was throbbing. I thought to myself, *Well, Brian, you finally pushed it too far this time!* I wasn't sure if I could continue on with the trip or not. I had never been so tired in my entire life. I had done what I set out to do—climb a mountain and live to tell about it. At that point I was ready to go back home. But I knew I couldn't give up. I knew I still had one more important task to accomplish in Peru.

Chapter Sixteen

COMPASSION DAY
WITH ROSA

On the final day of our trip to Peru, I woke up with a strange feeling of both excitement and terror. Three of the men on the trip had Compassion children in Peru. We made arrangements to meet these children on our last day. We decided to invite their entire families to join us for the day. We were going to spend the day at the Lima Zoo. As we left our hotel that morning, I was extremely nervous. I had been Rosa's Compassion sponsor for over five years. During that time we exchanged many letters and pictures. As we approached the entrance to the zoo, I felt like I was going to puke. I was more nervous to meet Rosa than I was to climb the mountain. What if she didn't like me? What if my disability scared her? What if she didn't even want to be there? As we stood at the front gates, I watched as the other two children arrived and met their sponsors. Finally Rosa pulled up and jumped out of the van. She was there with her mom, brother, and baby sister. As she exited the van, I limped over quickly to greet her. She had a huge smile on her face, and I grabbed her and gave her a huge hug. Although we needed an interpreter, our hearts and eyes said everything we needed to communicate with each other. I asked her questions as we walked "hand and hand" around the zoo. She had just had her birthday a few weeks earlier, but her mom said this was her "real birthday present." As we continued to talk, I found out how rare it was for a sponsored child to meet her Compassion Sponsor. I was told out of all the kids at her Compassion Project, only a few have ever had the opportunity to meet their sponsors. At that moment I realized what a gift it was to have this day with this precious family. As the day went on, Rosa and I continued to get closer and closer. I felt like she was one of my children. In fact I actually began sponsoring her before my own daughter was even born. We had a great day at the zoo and I was excited to see what God had in store for us.

Meeting my Compassion International sponsored
child Rosa for the first time.

Next, we all piled into the small vans and went to lunch together. We pulled into A fast food restaurant just down the road. It was obvious that most of these people had never been in a restaurant before. I was amazed at how they ate: they left nothing on their plates; they consumed every piece of food put in front of them. I could tell that they placed high value on food and did not want to waste anything. This made me think back on my own life. How many times have I been reckless and just thrown away food sitting my own plate? It made me sad and I felt terrible. After we finished eating, I watched as the families filled their purses and pockets with packets of ketchup and mustard. pockets with packets of ketchup and mustard. They were bringing anything they could back to their villages to share with the people in the community. It broke my heart to know how much I have been blessed with and how much I take for granted on a daily basis. After we finished eating, we went to the back of the restaurant where they had a play land set up for children to play. I spent a couple hours with Rosa in the ball pit and chasing her down the slides. The last 30 minutes of the day were my favorite. We got a chance to pray with each of the families and reflect on all that God has done in our lives. Then we exchanged gifts; prior to leaving for our trip, my wife and I bought some items to put in a backpack for Rosa. We had things like crayons, books, and an Ohio State sweat shirt. She loved it! She immediately got into the crayons and started making pictures. Then Rosa's mom gave me a gift. It was a handmade knitting cloth that said, "Happy Mother's Day!" I was blown away by the day and my emotions began to spill over. As we said our goodbyes, I hugged Rosa and did not want to let go. I promised her that I would be back and her mom said next time she wanted us to come to their home so she could cook for us. With tears in my eyes and a heavy heart, I said my final goodbye and embraced Rosa one last time. She got into a vehicle along with her family and headed back to her home. My last memory of my time with Rosa was her and her brother turning around in the car with big smiles on their faces, continuously waving at us until we were out of their sight. It was the perfect day. I looked forward to taking my own family to Peru one day soon so they could meet Rosa.

Recently I got some bad news: I found out that Rosa's Project had shut down and she no longer was part of Compassion International. This news devastated me. The thought of never seeing my extended

Peruvian family again was almost too much to take. I know in my heart that I will see Rosa again. I am already making plans for a return visit and have no doubt that God will allow our paths to cross again. Even if this was my only opportunity to meet Rosa, I am so grateful that God gave me the opportunity to have my life forever impacted by this amazing family and perfect day.

"My sweet Angel Rosa!" I will take this memory of us together wherever I go.

Chapter Seventeen

COMING HOME

I t was difficult returning home and trying to go back to any type of "normal life." My life had been greatly impacted in South America and I wanted to continue on that high. Through all the media attention leading up to our trip and the dramatic way it ended, many people and organizations asked me to speak at their locations. Public speaking was not something that I had envisioned doing, but I felt God was doing all these amazing things in my life and I wanted to praise him for that. At first, getting in front of people and talking about Jesus was difficult. I don't know if any of the great evangelists of the Bible had any issues when they first started speaking to people (something tells me Peter may have), but I sure did. It seemed like every time I had the opportunity to really glorify Jesus for what He had done in my life, I somehow always seemed to turn the attention back on myself. I guess I didn't realize how prideful I really was until I went back and looked at those first few speeches. Jesus should always be the "hero" of any sermon, and what I was doing was trying to put the attention meant for God and keep it for myself. This is probably why my first few public speaking events were absolute "train wrecks."

After a few more opportunities, I decided to spend more time preparing and in prayer before I opened my big fat mouth. This small change proved invaluable as I continued on with my speaking circuit over the next few months. One of the coolest places I got to speak at was the Refuge of Hope in Canton, Ohio. This was the homeless shelter were we had our Bible studies for the past year. Jason asked if I would be willing to share my testimony and help lead Bible study on Thursdays. I was nervous because these homeless dudes were really solid in their knowledge of the scriptures. I didn't want to get up there and sound like a total idiot. The first time I led the group, we looked at a passage from Mark's Gospel. After we finished up that night, I knew something inside of me had changed. I no longer was content with sitting on the sidelines. I wanted to get in the game and start telling people about Jesus Christ. I continued to help lead the Study for another few months, gaining valuable knowledge and building confidence each time.

I loved my time at the homeless shelter and we were continuing to grow our numbers each week. It was strange: just when we were at our peak at the Refuge, I felt this strong feeling that God wanted me to do the same thing in my hometown. I prayed about it for a while and after getting God's affirmation, decided to start the same type of "community" in my hometown—Massillon. I had spent so much time in discipleship relationships with men in the city that I had neglected my most important disciples, my family. I wanted to create an environment where my family and I could grow closer together and help bring our friends and family to Christ. Our final night at the shelter was amazing. We had a baptism ceremony in the parking lot and the men of Refuge helped send us off to our new destination. It was an emotional night and a big part of me did not want to leave. I knew that we had to; God was calling me out of my comfort zone and placing me into a community that desperately needed to hear the "Good News of Jesus Christ."

After a year in Massillon, we started one large "community" and three small "discipleship groups." I was blown away by what God was doing in the lives of our family and friends. It was evident that we made the right decision. This city needed a change—we needed a change. We needed to change the way people viewed ministry and start to invest in people and relationships, not buildings and programs.

This was an extremely busy time in my life. Since I cannot do anything the easy way, I decided to complicate my life even more. I got a new job at a large corporation in the area. This job was such a blessing because it gave my wife and me the opportunity to be faithful to our church with tithing, and we were able to get two more Compassion children. This new place of employment also gave their employees the opportunity to go back to school and get their degrees. I knew that I needed to finish my degree. While I was at college playing basketball, I only took classes that would keep me eligible. My class load was full of intense courses like volleyball, basketball officiating, and history of rock n roll. It seemed like a good idea at the time, but colleges don't really look too highly on these classes.

I decided I wanted to attend Malone University and major in project management. The program was fourteen months long and took up a lot of my time. It was an accelerated program that was incremented into six-week modules. I was excited to start the program because I knew getting my degree was something that I needed to have, and I wanted my daughter to know that although her daddy had to overcome many obstacles in his life, he was still able to get a job, serve God, and get his degree. After a few weeks into the program, I realized that I had completely underestimated the time commitment that getting this degree would require. I was working almost 50 hours a week, leading this new ministry in Massillon, and trying to find time to do homework. On top of all that, I still had all of my health issues that I had to deal with.

That was a difficult year but eventually I made it through and got my degree. I was excited and since I have "ministry ADD," I decided to do something fun and borderline crazy to glorify Jesus. I heard about this organization called the Christian Children's Home of Ohio (CCHO). It was an organization that helped bring healing to hurting children through foster and adoption placements. We decided it would be awesome to capitalize on the momentum we had gained from our mountain climbing experience in Peru. I decided to organize another fundraiser in order to raise money and awareness for the children at CCHO. After talking with some of my ministry friends, we organized a team that was willing to climb 40 miles in three days along the Appalachian Trail. I partnered with Rivertree Christian Church and an organization called Climbing 4 Kids with the goal of raising $10,000.

I had never been to the Appalachian Trail before, but I figured I just climbed a mountain, so *how tough could it actually be?* We spent the next month hitting up our friends and family trying to hit our goal of 10k. The week before we were scheduled to leave, I got the email telling me we had hit our goal and reached our pledge amount. I was really encouraged by the amount of support we had received.

The day of the climb started early in the morning. We left around 4:00 AM on Friday morning. The plan was to catch the Appalachian Trail near Harrisburg, PA. Once we arrived we had to check in with the local Ranger Station. I guess hikers are encouraged to do this so they can keep track of you in the event one of us got lost. As we were speaking to the woman at the Ranger Post, she began asking us questions like, "Have you ever been to the AT before?" and "Do you know how to read trail markers?" Of course our answer was "NO" to both her questions, and I began to see a sense of worry come across her face. Apparently, people actually prepare to hike the Appalachian Trail, not just show up and try to "wing it." We asked her for some "pointers" and she was nice enough to help us out. I know that this lady was fairly confident that one of us was going to get lost or injured on the trail because her final words to us were, "Please don't make us come and look for you guys." With that vote of confidence, we unloaded our vehicle and began the first leg of our 40-mile trek through Eastern PA.

As we began our hike, the first thing I noticed was that this was way harder than I had envisioned. I did do a little research on the trail before we left, and this part of the AT was considered "moderate." I guess that classification only holds true if you are young and in shape. By the end of day one we were all exhausted. I remember walking to our campsite and none of us were talking. After day one we had only finished 12 miles and the consensus with the rest of my team was there was no way we were going to hit 40. This was not a positive sign for the rest of the weekend. After we had made it back safely to the campsite, the first thing I did was take off my shoes. The hardest part of hiking this part of the trail was dealing with the rocks. These rocks were monsters: some of them were big (I had to literally roll my body over top of them), and some were jagged (like little daggers that were jamming into your feet after each step). The trail itself was also difficult to navigate. I guess I was expecting an actual trail (like the name implies). Not so much; this "trail" was narrow in some areas, steep in others, and completely washed out in some places. It was really hard to stay on task and if it would have rained, it would have been impossible for us to hike.

We started out the next day with an optimistic attitude. Instead of looking at it as one big day (Saturday), I chose to break it into chunks, morning and afternoon. During our morning hike, we covered 10 miles of rough AT terrain. As we sat together at lunch, I told the guys that I wanted to get another 15 miles in before the end of the day. It was difficult but by the time we went to bed Saturday night, we had completed 25 miles. I remember sitting by the campfire that night with my team. We could hardly keep our eyes open; our bodies had been pushed to the limit, but we were determined to finish the 40 miles for the children. That night as I fell asleep staring at the beautiful night sky, I was overwhelmed with emotion. I couldn't believe how God was continuing to show up in my life and all the amazing things He was doing. Here I was on my second major climb in two years, raising money for some hurting children and getting to spend the weekend with a bunch of guys who loved Jesus.

Sunday morning we woke up early to finish the last leg of our hike. It was an easy five miles and we had the opportunity to relax and take some photos. As we walked to the van, the insanity of the weekend started to take its toll on us. We loaded up our gear and made our way down the interstate towards home. An hour into our ride, we stopped to get something to eat at one of those travel plazas. As I exited the car and tried to take my first step, I got my first glimpse of what 40 miles on the Appalachian Trail could do to a person. I dragged my body across the parking lot and into the plaza. I could feel everyone looking at me trying to figure out what the heck was wrong with me. I thought I was tired after Machu Picchu, but this took pain to a whole new level. Every part of my body was aching. After we finally made it back home, I spent the next two days in bed trying to recuperate from the severe "body whipping" the Appalachian Trail put on me.

A few weeks later after we had collected all our pledges and donations, we were invited to CCHO for a party to celebrate our achievement. I was really excited for this because I wanted the chance to meet some of the kids we were raising money for. We had a cookout before the ceremony, and my wife and I sat with a group of young foster children. As we sat together and ate, the children started to share some of their stories with us. It made me sad and angry to hear what these children had to endure in just their first few years of life. I heard stories of abuse, neglect and drugs; I became more enraged after each story. I couldn't believe that a parent could put a child through such terrible tragedy. I remember one young girl shared with me that her mother was involved with witchcraft and was forcing her to be a part of it. This little girl knew it was wrong and started to read the Bible all by herself. After she was taken away from her parents, she decided she wanted to become a priest. I was amazed at her knowledge of the scriptures. She knew the Bible better than most adults. She recited story after story and told me her favorite book in the Bible was Ruth. I told her how proud I was of her and that I would be praying for her.

Once we finished eating, we moved the party inside to the Retreat Center. As the ceremony began, I was excited to share what God had done by raising all this money. As I began to speak, I planned on talking about how cool our trip was and sharing a few stories from the weekend. But as I was speaking, my focus switched and I started to share with the audience how God was changing my heart and I felt like He wanted my wife and me to pray about fostering a child of our own. I remember telling them, "I started out with the mindset of how I can help these hurting children, but it ended up being how these amazing children can help me." A few months later, my wife and I began the process of becoming licensed foster parents.

Chapter Eighteen

BROTHER FROM A
DIFFERENT FATHER

The more I follow God, the more I am convinced He has a fanatical sense of humor. Around the same time that we were getting licensed to foster or adopt a child, I got some unexpected news that would change my life (for the better) forever.

One afternoon, my wife was visiting a family member who was recovering from an illness. This woman was not doing well, so the doctor gave her some medication that took away her pain. As she was talking to my wife, she kept referencing "the baby." After a few more slipups, she let loose the bomb shell: she said when my mother was really young, she had a baby. She knew she couldn't take care of the child, so she made the difficult choice to place him up for adoption. I am sure there is a lot more to this story that I will ever find out.

What do you do with news like that? I got a call later that day from my wife. I could tell she needed to tell me something but was nervous to deliver the message. When she finally told me what happened, I felt numb. I couldn't believe what she was telling me. I thought to myself, *No way, not my family—I knew everything about my mother!* The more she told me, the worse I felt. Not for me, but for my mom and my brother who never had the opportunity to meet his fantastic mother. I imagined how hard it must have been for my mom to have that baby and then give it to another family to raise. I know my mother's heart had to have been broken. I often think about what that day would have been like. Did my mom get to hold her baby? Did she get the opportunity to meet the family who was adopting her baby boy? What was the last thing she said to him?

A few days later, my family member called me over to her home and we talked about the situation. I love this woman; she is an amazing person and we had a great relationship through the years. I listened intently as she told me what happened. She told me a little about the family who adopted him. She asked me to please keep this a secret and do not reach out to him. I left her house sad. How could I not reach out to my brother? He was my own flesh and blood. I thought long and hard about what my mom would have wanted me to do. I prayed and asked God to help me make the right decision. I wanted to honor my family, but I had to do what I knew was right in my heart. I thought about my mother; I thought about her walking in Heaven with Jesus. What would she want me to do? After that, I knew what I needed to do: even though I would suffer serious repercussions from my family, I had to find my big brother—it's what my mom would want me to do.

Before leaving her house, I was able to find out when my brother was born and what hospital it was at. That was more than enough information for my wife—she went "MacGyver style" trying to locate my lost brother. She started looking online at all the adoption forums she could find. I think it may have only taken a day and my wife had already located him. She found a site where people who have been adopted can post their birth information in hopes of finding their biological families. Suzie was able to match up the same birth date and hospital with a man who was looking for family. We got his name and started to look for him on social media. Eventually we were able to get a phone number for his brother who lived in Las Vegas. Now the situation just got real. I was so scared to call this man. What would I say to him? How would I explain the situation? What if my brother didn't want to be found? Finally I got up the nerve to call. I did my best to explain to him what was going on. I braced myself to get screamed at or even threatened. Instead, I got a shocked, curious, and encouraging response from him. We talked for a while and he told me a bit about my brother. I found out my new brother is really smart; he got his degree and moved to Washington, DC, to work. I also found out that he had recently moved back to Ohio and was living 30 minutes away. I couldn't believe how this was working out and how easy everything seemed to be progressing. As we were wrapping up the conversation, I asked him to give my brother my number. I said, "If he wants to call me I would love to talk, but I understand if he would rather not." I wasn't sure if he would call. Later on that evening I got my answer: the phone rang. It was him—my long lost big brother.

We talked for an hour or so about everything. I told him all about his family and what we were doing with our lives. I was excited to fill him in on all the little details about our family. Then he asked the question I had neglected to put much thought into: "So, is Mom still alive?" With a heavy heart, I told him that Mom had died a few years ago. I know part of him was disappointed. I'm sure he would have loved to meet his bio mother. I am sure Mom would have loved to meet him, too. He took the news in stride. He told me about his amazing family and what it was like for him growing up. It made me feel good to know he was happy. We had a few more conversations over the next few weeks. We talked about getting together, maybe going out to dinner sometime.

We agreed to meet up for breakfast. My sister and I met my new brother at a small dinner in downtown Akron. As soon as I saw him for the first time, I knew we were related. He looked just like me. We gave each other a hug and sat down to talk. We talked about doing a DNA test but we knew there was no need—we looked so much alike. We brought some family pictures so he could see what Mom looked like. We had a great time and made plans to see each other again soon. We have kept in touch and continue to see each other once or twice a year.

I don't think it's any coincidence that as Suzie and I were starting down the path of foster/adoption, God chose to reveal to me my brother and his adoption story. I know that Jesus was preparing our hearts with our experience with the children of CCHO and all the information we received in our adoption classes. I used to think these types of events were just random and had nothing at all to do with God and His ultimate plan for our lives. The further along I go in my walk with Christ, I realize that God doesn't do random: everything He does He does for a reason. Yea, it sucks that I got in a car accident and was paralyzed, but He is using it to bring people closer to Him. And it's not fair that my mom had to die at such a young age, unable to see her kids get married or enjoy all her grandchildren, but I know God will use that tragedy to do something awesome. I used to hate when people would use the phrase, "We don't understand why God did what He did, but it happened for a reason." That felt like a "cop out" answer. I wanted facts! I wanted God to come down to earth and tell me personally why He decided to completely upend someone's life (this is before I read the story of Job). Now years later, I figured that everything God does fits together in His "master plan." All of life's joys, trials, and triumphs are like little puzzle pieces that fit together and help shape our lives and build up the Kingdom of God.

Chapter Nineteen

YOU BETTER LIVE IT OUT

N ot long after meeting my brother, Suzie and I finished our classes and officially became licensed foster parents. One of the first things you do when you are finishing up your home study is to fill out a child "wish list." This is probably not the correct term for this process, but it's a pretty accurate description. My wife and I sat down with our social worker and filled out this long checklist for the type of child we would be willing to accept into our home. We were fairly certain of the "perfect child" we wanted to foster. We were looking for a baby (0–12 months), no sexual abuse, doesn't hit, has no mental issues, and definitely no children older than our biological child Kaymen. Sounds like a pretty good list, right? Do you know what God thinks of lists like this?

A few months later my wife called me at work and told me about a dream she had the night before. She said she dreamed we adopted two children, one older boy and a younger girl. Later on that day I got another call from Suzie, this time her voice a lot more frantic. She had gotten a call from our case worker asking if we would be willing to foster (you guessed it) two children. The boy was seven years old and the little girl was five. We didn't get much information on either child. We had no idea what these kids had been through and what they would be like in our home. We had to make a decision quickly (because for some reason every decision a foster parent makes needs to happen that very second). We thought and prayed about it. I thought back to "my list": just about everything I checked a "no" for we were getting with these two kids. How in the world were we going to do this? Just then I thought back to my wife's dream. Was God trying to tell us something? After all that I had been through and everything Jesus was doing in my life, I was not about to question the validity of this dream. It was all the assurance I needed. It was self-examination time: "Do you really trust God or not?" If you really believe in this Jesus stuff, you better live it out!

Later on that day we were in the car on our way to pick up two new additions to our family. I tried to mentally prepare myself for what was about to take place. How were they going to handle the reality that they were about to get into a vehicle with total strangers and drive 45 minutes away to go and live with them? As we pulled up to the back of the building, I saw two kids standing near the entrance. The little boy was curious about who we were, but was more concerned with playing with the other children. The little girl was crying loudly and refused to leave the other foster mother's arms. I had absolutely no idea what to do or what to say. Luckily my wife took charge and grabbed the girl and put her into the car (immediately she calmed down). I heard the boy blurt out a statement I have become so familiar with hearing, "Hey, what's wrong with that guy's leg?"

As we were loading up the car, the "reality" of the situation started to resonate inside of me: each child only had one garbage bag full of clothes. "One bag—this is all they have?" I threw the bags in the trunk and prepared for the ride home. I could tell quickly that this wasn't the first time that these children had been in foster care. They were not yelling or screaming, they just asked a lot of questions. They wanted to know where we lived and what we had at our home. I thought about my own daughter and how she would react if she were in the car with complete strangers. I couldn't believe how calm they were. It's almost like this was their reality, this is all they knew.

Adjusting to life with two traumatized children was difficult. We learned quickly that these kids were not like my bio daughter and they had some serious issues. One of the biggest challenges to deal with was the fact that they would not sleep. After we tucked them in to their beds, they decided it was time to get up and roam the house. If they did manage to stay in bed for any extended period of time, they would "yell out" for us in the middle of the night. After 48 hours of this (along with numerous other issues) I had enough. I called our worker and told her this was not going to work out. The next day our living room was full of county and agency workers trying to convince me to "hold on" a little longer. I was done. I was ready to ship these kids back to the county and let someone else deal with their problems. I must have told them three different times that I wanted the children removed and each time they avoided my statement. I could tell they had been through this before and knew I was a scared "first time" foster parent. By the end of the meeting they had convinced me to give it one more day. I agreed but told them to "stay close to the phone" in case I called.

The next day I decided to take the family to the Akron Zoo. I figured maybe a change in environment would do us all some good. I also thought it would be a nice memory for these children because I planned on them leaving the following morning. As we began our walk around the penguin aquarium, I felt my attitude towards these kids start to change. I had conversations with them. They started to open up more about what they had been through. They were just kids laughing, playing, and having a great time. By the end of the day I was holding both my little girls' hands and answering the million different questions my foster son was firing at me. We had a great day and for the first time I thought to myself, *Hey, this whole foster thing may work out.* I called the county worker when I got home and told her I wanted to give it a little more time. I am fairly confident that this woman probably fell out of her chair when I told her the news, considering I was demanding these children be removed from my home the day before.

For the next six months life was great. We had virtually no problems with the children. I remember telling people that "we hit the lotto" when it came to foster kids. I was excited for my family and the possibility of adding these two precious souls to our family permanently. We were finally settling into a place where we were all comfortable. Well, if I have learned one thing about God, it's that He is not a big fan of His followers living a "comfortable" lifestyle.

As I awoke that Christmas morning, I went into my foster daughter's room to wake her up. She was extremely agitated and was not acting like the little girl I had grown to know over the past few months. After opening presents and eating breakfast, her attitude turned from unpleasant to downright nasty. I asked her what was wrong and why she was acting this way. Her response back to me was that she wanted to "ruin Christmas for the entire family." I didn't think much of it at the time because I just figured it was the holidays and she was missing her family and didn't know how to appropriately say what she was feeling. My hope was that after a few days, she would snap out of it and turn back into her normal self.

As the months went by, her behavior continued to get worse. It began with simple actions like lying, manipulating, and temper tantrums. Once she figured out she could get our attention by acting this way, her behavior got much worse. By the time spring rolled around, this sweet innocent child was out of control. She was claiming to have conversations with the devil. She was having thoughts about hurting our family. She even began acting out inappropriately and was called down to the principal's office for telling the gym teacher all about the various traumas she had been through as a child. Not long after all this, she began to make false accusations about other children and myself. One day she came home from school and informed me she had told her teacher that I had done all kinds of inappropriate things towards her (insert every foster parent's worst fear). I had to call the sheriff and try to explain to him that I have a traumatized six-year-old foster child in my house who likes to make up stories to get other people in trouble. Not one of my top ten phone calls I have ever had to make.

We tried everything we could think of to try and get this little girl the help she so desperately needed. We went to multiple counselors, doctors, and psychiatrists. Each time we went they gave us a different diagnosis. One evening, this little girl could no longer control her emotions. After an altercation at one of her doctor's visits, she came home in a violent mood. I was having trouble keeping her calm and she was not staying in her room. After a half hour of trying to diffuse the situation, my worst fear came true. She went into the kitchen, grabbed a knife, and told me she was going to cut her wrists. I couldn't believe I was watching a six-year-old girl do this. I will never get that image out of my head. She was in complete terror and had no idea what to do to make things better. I had to act fast because the other two children were in the backyard playing and had no idea what was taking place. After pleading with her for a while, I finally got her to put the knife away. It was at this point that I knew I could no longer take care of this fragile little child. She needed help and she needed it fast. I knew the next time she attempted something like this she would take it even further.

The next day I called our social worker and told her that we needed to find a place that could give this girl the kind of help she needed. I asked that she be placed in a treatment facility for a few months and then, if she got better, she could return back home to us. The county decided it would be in her best interest not to be placed in a treatment facility, but instead be placed with another foster family who could devote their sole attention on her. This news was devastating to my wife and me. We had spent over a year with this child. She had become my daughter. I felt terrible for her brother. This was the only family he had and now she was being taking from him. I felt a huge sense of guilt. *If only I had handled things differently. If I would have gotten her into the right doctor maybe they would have helped her.* These thoughts began to haunt me. I felt a huge sense of responsibility for this girl and now she was being moved.

I truly believe that God reveals himself through children. The night before my foster daughter was scheduled to leave our home, I saw a glimpse of Jesus. After we finished eating, I called the whole family over to the couch. My wife and I then proceeded to do our best to explain to this little child that she would be leaving our home and going to live with complete strangers. It was the hardest conversation I have ever had. Once we finished up, this little child looked up at me with tears in her eyes and said, "Don't cry, Daddy. I know this is my fault. Everything will work out!" I couldn't believe what I just heard. I thought I was going to be the one doing the consoling, not the other way around. We spent the rest of the night looking at pictures and talking about what this "new future" for our family will be like. Before we went to bed, my wife asked her if she would like Daddy to baptize her. I had no idea what type of family she was going to and didn't have a clue if they believed in Jesus or not. So at 9:00 PM I filled up the bathroom tub and baptized my foster daughter. It was one of the most impactful, powerful, and real moments of my entire life.

The next day a county worker showed up at our home and loaded all of this little girl's belongings into a van and drove off. I looked at my wife and she was in tears. I tried to reassure myself that this was the right decision. I did everything I could to convince our family that we would still have a relationship with her, that she would just be living in a different home. I knew in my mind that this was the best decision for our family, but in my heart I felt like a failure. How could I do this to her? How could I do this to her brother? I reflected back to the promise I made to her dad a few months earlier. We had gotten close to him and he gave me his blessing to raise his little girl—how could I abandon her? This is not the picture-perfect ending I envisioned when I decided to foster a child.

Over the next few months my family went through all kinds of emotions. We needed to heal but there was a lot of sadness, guilt, and anger that we needed to work through. My wife cried a lot. She felt terrible that we could not keep this little girl in our home. I was so proud of the effort and commitment my wife made to trying to make the situation better. Over the fourteen months that this little girl was in our home, my wife did everything possible to help this little girl overcome her issues. She spent countless hours driving her to different appointments in hopes that some new doctor had the "magic answer" to help her get better. I admired Suzie's determination; when everyone was telling us that our little girl was "unfixable," Suzie refused to give up. She gave everything she had up until the day that our little girl left our house. It killed me to watch helplessly as my wife slipped into depression. It didn't matter that she was only in our home for fourteen months, this was our daughter and it was agonizing for a mother to have her little girl taken from our home.

While my wife was dealing with extreme sadness, I was the opposite and I was trying to handle the fact that I was extremely angry about the situation. Although I loved this little girl with all my heart, I was very angry at her and had a lot of rage towards her and what she put our family through over the past year. I know that she is only a child and had no control over her actions, but I was having trouble getting my emotions under control. Up until this point in my life, I had really never had any issues with anger. I found myself getting into altercations with my wife on an almost daily basis. I was yelling at my kids for the tiniest of infractions. I was angry with my job. I was frustrated with my ministries. To top it all, I started to have suicidal thoughts. Not all the time, but they were becoming more and more frequent. The stress of everything our family had been through over the last year was too much for me to deal with by myself. I needed help.

After some pushing from my wife, I finally agreed to go and talk to a counselor. I was really hesitant to go at first. I told my wife that I could take care of my problems by myself. I mean I had everything I needed, my Bible and Jesus. I quickly realized that although those are extremely powerful tools, there are times in life when you need to turn to other believers to help you get through the difficult times. After a few sessions, it was apparent that I was really "screwed up" and needed some help to get back on track. I believe that God is the ultimate sculptor; He continues to chip away at our hearts to turn us into the people who He created us to be. As prideful, sinful humans, we do our best to keep Jesus away from our hearts because we don't want to change; we like the way we are. But if we can surrender ourselves to Christ, He will strip all the "bad stuff" out of our lives and start to chisel away our hearts. That's what He is doing with me and that's what He wants to do with you!

Chapter Twenty

MY NEXT THIRTY YEARS!

I figure every experience I have encountered over the last thirty-seven years has been preparing me for this next stage of my life. Of all the really cool things God has allowed me to do, what I enjoy best is telling others about Jesus. I have had numerous opportunities to share my testimony with different groups. Each time I get to speak about what God has done in my life, I use it as an opportunity to sharpen my message and refine my skills. One of the things I really feel like God is calling me to do at this point in my life is to speak. I have been blessed to have some amazing pastor friends who open their churches to me and give me the chance to deliver sermons. I love to do this because I want my life and my story to be more than just my accident. I want to be able to get up in front of a group of people and point them to Jesus through my words and my life. This has not come easy to me. I have learned to study scripture and seek the advice of some solid theologians whom I trust and love. I know what a responsibility it is to stand in front of a church and teach, I don't take this lightly.

Besides speaking at churches, I have also embraced the idea of living out my life missionally. It's important that we show up on

Sunday mornings and fellowship at church with other believers. But I believe that God is more interested in how our lives look Monday–Saturday. It's one thing to act holy at church on Sunday morning, but how are you acting Monday morning at the office? I want to make sure that my life lines up with what God expects out of one of His followers. This is basically how our "community" Massillon Village was formed. A group of people on mission to help each other do "life together." This is just a fancy way of saying that we are committed to living as a community of believers who are dedicated to holding each other accountable to God's Word (and no, we are not a cult!).

Someone once asked me what my "spiritual gift" was; I had absolutely no idea what he was talking about. After nearly ten years of following Jesus, I think I finally figured it out. I'm an evangelist. I love to have conversations with people about Jesus and help them turn their lives towards the cross. As much as I am ashamed of many events that happened in my past, I realized that it is one of my greatest gifts. I am relatable to the average person. Just like Paul was an apostle to the Gentiles and Peter was an apostle to the Jews, I have a unique audience who I am able to reach because of my past experiences. I am realistic about it, too. I have tattoos all over my body, I love to hang out with ex-drug addicts and gang members, and I like to have an occasional whiskey and soda. I'm probably not going to be invited to be the keynote speaker at many hyperspiritual Jesus events, but I am useful. I have a purpose. There are people out there that I can reach. We all have specific audiences who we can impact. It may be your family, friends, or your coworkers. It's important for us to know our "battleground" so we can spread "God's Word" in an effective way. Bringing people to Christ is not some magic formula or program, it's accomplished through relationships. It's entering into a meaningful relationship with someone and allowing them to experience Christ through and with you. Making disciples is not easy. It's messy and at times inconvenient. None of us have an extra hour to carve out of our lives, but if you are serious about making an impact for Jesus, you need to make time. When I enter into a discipleship relationship with someone, my cell phone is always on. It's impossible to set boundaries (i.e., you can only call me from 8:00 AM – 8:00 PM). That's not realistic; the reason they need Jesus in the first place is because their life is a mess. If you're not willing to pick up your phone at 2:00 AM, every once in a while you should reexamine your priorities. I am still learning about Jesus, but I am fairly confident if He had a cell phone He would be available anytime day or night.

One of the most important points I try and emphasize whenever I speak is that you don't have to have some amazing testimony or really cool story to bring people to Christ. I have much more respect for people who have been lifelong faithful servants of Jesus than I do for the person who comes to Christ from some miraculous event. Stories like mine happen all the time. It's easy to live a life full of sin. It's heroic to live a life full of Jesus!

So here I am sixteen years after my accident and my life has been transformed. I would never have dreamed that my life would turn out this way, but I am so grateful that God never gave up on me. Before my accident I thought I had life figured out. I planned on playing basketball professionally, maybe getting married, and living down South. That was my plan—God had a different plan, a better plan in mind for me. A plan that involved taking an arrogant, selfish, and mean young man and turning him into a tool to bring people to Christ.

Although God has done some incredible healing in my life, my body is still a battered, broken, beaten down shell of its old self. I wake up every day and have to drag myself out of bed and into the shower. After I take my cocktail of muscle relaxants and let the warm water ease the severe spasms that are taking my body captive, I limp my way over to the floor to begin my stretching exercises for the day. This will continue on every day until the day I die. I will never get better—I will gradually get worse. There is no surgery or pill to slow down the eventual reality that my body is headed back to the place I fought so hard to get out of—a wheelchair. I fight every day. I try not to complain. I have accepted and embraced the reality that I am a quadriplegic and will continue to battle obstacles the rest of my life. I refuse to let this paralysis define who I am or what I can accomplish. I continue to set crazy, high, lofty goals and will kill myself trying to attain them. There are days that I hate life. I get sick of going through this daily routine just to drag myself to work every day and sit at a desk for 10 ½ hours. There are days that I long for death. Not because I want to die or leave my family, but because I am ready to go home and be with my Heavenly Father.

Bringing the Good News of Jesus Christ has become the sole reason for my existence. I am prepared to live and die for Christ! I continue to study the Bible and try my best to live in a way that would honor God. Each day I fall more and more in love with Jesus. I take His last words on earth very seriously (I even have them tattooed on my wrist showing Mark 16:15–18). The "Great Commission" is not just scripture to me, it is instruction; a guide that makes this seemingly meaningless life have a purpose. As followers of Jesus our job is to continue to make disciples. It's a lifelong process that God expects us to live out every day.

Each day brings a new opportunity for us. An opportunity to share what God has done for us in our own lives and the amazing gift He gave us on the cross. I don't want to waste a single day. Luther puts it best: *"You are not only responsible for what you say, but also what you do not say!"* Throughout this process I have come to realize that there are times that life sucks! It's hard and can be overwhelming. This was not God's intent when He created the world. As I read through Genesis and the story of Adam and Eve, I wonder what it would have been like to live in Eden. Imagine living without sin or pain and having complete access to God himself. What an amazing image! Unfortunately Satan screwed that up for all of us. Now we have to come to terms that we live in a world that is full of hurt, pain, and sin. But this was not God's intent. He is not an angry disciplinarian that actively looks for opportunities to punish people. He is a loving father who wants to see His children become all that He created them to be. So along the way, bad things are going to happen to us—FACT! How we respond to those trials is a true measure of how much we trust and love Jesus. For me I'm paralyzed, and that really stinks, but this is not the worst event that will happen in my life. Through reading the scriptures, praying, and the community of believers I've surrounded myself with, I've tried to equip myself as best I can to deal with the next crisis that will no doubt come my way.

If you're reading this and you're dealing with a struggle in your life that is overwhelming and it feels like there is no hope; or you're reading this and you feel as though you are just walking aimlessly through this life with no real purpose or direction, I want you to remember one important fact: **God does not want you to live a paralyzed life!** He wants you to get out there and enjoy His creation. He wants you to live life to the fullest. He wants you to go on amazing adventures and experience the agape love that He has for each one of His children. God has a plan for your life. I'm living proof. Jesus met me in my darkest, loneliest hour and gave me what we all desire most—HOPE—and He longs to do the same in your life.

Through this journey in life, I realized that at some point in all our lives each and every one of us is eventually brought to our knees. We have to ask ourselves the universal question that's been asked for thousands of years: WHY? Why is this terrible illness happening to me? Why did I lose my job? Why did my family member have to die?

Although this book may not answer the "why" question, my hope and prayer is that after reading this, it may help lead you to the one person who can help answer that question—Jesus Christ.